CLASSROOM
DISPLAY

Improving the visual environment in schools

Noel Hodgson

Tarquin Publications

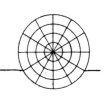

Noel Hodgson studied at Leeds College of Art where he took the Diploma of Art and Design. From there he went to Goldsmiths College, London to earn his Art Teacher's Certificate.

After his apprenticeship at Balmoral School, Morecambe (now Heysham High School) he moved on to Ribblesdale School, Clitheroe, where he is now head of Design Studies and is developing courses in Design and Technology.

A year's secondment allowed him to gain an Advanced Certificate in Craft Design and Technology at Edge Hill College, Ormskirk.

Acknowledgements
A book like this owes much to the inspiration of others and I should like to acknowledge the help given to me by family, friends and colleagues. I have also been greatly helped by many of the shopkeepers of Clitheroe, with particular thanks going to Ethos Galleries D. Byrne & Co., K. D. Bookshop, Allen's Paint Store, G. B. Paper Plus and the Skipton Building Society.
My colleagues Alyson Hobin and Jem Lees have kindly helped with artwork, especially that on page 82.
Clive Tallon, the computer wizard, has helped greatly with the section on computer graphics.

Special thanks for help and permission to use photographs and art work from:-

Brookside County Primary School, Clitheroe
Edisford County Primary School, Clitheroe
Primet High School, Colne
Ribblesdale County Secondary School, Clitheroe
Dobroyd Castle School (as it was then), Todmorden
Didsbury College of Higher Education, Manchester
Edgehill College of Higher Education, Ormskirk
Lancashire Polytechnic, Preston
Blackburn Teachers' Centre
Burnley Curriculum Development Centre.

To Nicholas Jenkins, who wrestled with the manuscript and finally made the publication of this book possible

---

I.S.B.N. 0 906212 62 6

Editor: Nicholas Jenkins
Design: Philip Streeting
Printing: The Five Castles Press Limited, Ipswich

Tarquin Publications
Stradbroke
Diss
Norfolk IP21 5JP
England

CONTENTS

"The best days of your life?"

THE VISUAL ENVIRONMENT

This book is a do-it-yourself guide to display for teachers. I've written it because I believe strongly in the importance of the visual environment in schools. It is not simply a question of hanging pictures straight (although I have some ideas to share with you in that direction), but in creating a 'look' or visual 'atmosphere' within the school which helps to encourage high morale and enthusiasm. From my own practical experience, an exciting visual environment stimulates children's interest and imagination and raises standards throughout the school. Enthusiastic staff make for interested children. Interested children make it easier for staff to be enthusiastic and to enjoy their work. It is this benevolent interaction, a 'virtuous spiral', which we wish to encourage.

There are very many complex interactions and influences between children, staff and parents which help all to feel that their school is indeed a 'good' school. It is the contention of this book that one of these influences is the quality of the visual environment. I think that it is an important influence and that it is one which is relatively easy to improve and change.

Let me show you what I mean.

Let us take an imaginary walk around an imaginary school. We shan't give it a name, although we can all name schools like it. What impressions do we get when we see the front gate? Remember that to most people, this is about as much of the school as they will ever see. Let us go inside.

The corridors are dark and draughty. The notice-board and display areas are mostly empty. Just one tatty poster advertises an event which took place six months ago.

Let us look inside an empty classroom.

There is nothing except a calendar on the wall. No clue as to what the children are doing. No idea whose classroom it is. A transit camp on the way to nowhere?

Do these bookshelves suggest a school which is dynamic and enthusiastic?

Of course, just as good advertising does not guarantee a good product, so it is possible that this school churns out an unending stream of scholars and saints.

That is not the issue. The question is to wonder if they might be more scholarly and more saintly if the visual environment were better?

Is it possible that behaviour is influenced by the visual environment?

Here's a corridor which creates a rather different impression. Don't be distracted by their angelic smiles! Look how the corridor is framed by a continuous wall display. What's more, the pictures are not there by accident. They have been consciously placed there to create a clean and tidy effect. They also emphasise continuity and links with the past. You may now look at the angels — see, they're clean and tidy! Is this a coincidence?

This is a close up of one of the items in the 'life and times' display which lines the corridor above. It's nothing spectacular in itself, as you can see, but it's an integral part of the overall effect. This is one of the essences of display skills: the blending and harmonising of small units to make each unit appear somehow more significant than at first it might appear. We've only reached page 7 of the book, but I hope you are already racking your brains. Can you see your own school with the eyes of an outsider or a casual visitor?

What impression does it give to parents who are thinking of sending their children to your school?

Does your school own any original prints or works by local artists which could be framed for the entrance hall or corridors? Do you have any original editions of newspapers when your school (or perhaps a distinguished ex-pupil) hit the headlines? Can the visual environment be improved?

This display, which is an attractive feature of Brookside Primary School, is a good example of a permanent display which always remains topical. The coloured markers show where all the children live and it is updated whenever someone leaves or a new pupil arrives. It brings a new dimension to a 'change of address' card!

It was a lot of work to make this board originally, but it is a continuing source of interest and constantly reinforces the links between the school and the community.

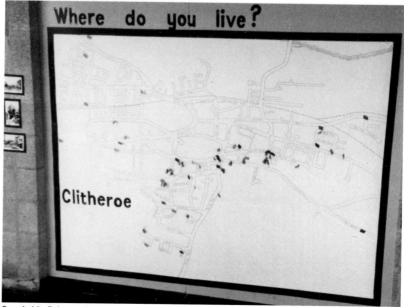

Brookside Primary School

The displays overleaf were essentially long-term and thus were solidly made and properly framed. Most displays within a classroom are of much shorter duration. They must last long enough to state the importance of the work displayed, but then be taken down and changed. Think of a display not as an artifact but as a process. Once people start to take it for granted then it should be changed. The picture on the right certainly outlasted its usefulness and the card frame began to look tatty. Soon after this photograph was taken, the frame was removed to the incinerator!

Display at its simplest is to pin interesting material to the notice-boards which already exist within the classrooms or elsewhere in the school.

The notice-board on the left derives most of its source material from our 'unsolicited mail-bag', whereas the one below features professionally produced sheets and cuttings.

The results speak for themselves. Hand on heart, are your notice boards as effective as these?

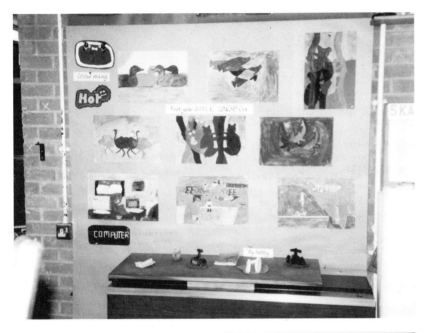

The presentation of the pupils' own work is the mainstay of display up to middle school level. But in the realm of art and craft, it remains vitally important for pupils of all levels and ages. These skills are fundamental to GCSE art exams, and whatever subject you teach, it is likely that you will find pupils who would like to help you with your displays.

This superb display on the left demonstrates what can be achieved. Its creator has a passion for pop music, as you can see, but even the most dedicated Radio 3 listener could not fail to take notice. If the imaginary classroom we entered a few pages ago had displays like the ones pictured here on its walls, how differently might we have reacted?

Display skills may be learned in the art room but they can and should be exercised throughout the school. A surprising number of children are capable of mounting first rate displays when given a little help and encouragement. I have found that when I have to put on some sort of classroom exhibition, I am able to rely on these young enthusiasts to do the detailed lay-out leaving me free to co-ordinate the overall 'feel' of the room.

You must get into the habit of being something of a magpie. And make sure none of your friends and colleagues ever throws anything out without your written permission! You must then collect material into resource files. I've lost count of how many different files I keep, but my 'image bank' (as I call it) contains files on such subjects as 'Animals', 'Looking Good', 'Beautiful Britain' etc. I haven't yet got one on 'Zebras' or 'Zanzibar'! Each is made up from newspaper cuttings, advertisements, travel brochures, colour supplement pictures, free hand-outs and sometimes photographs taken by myself and colleagues. As well as these I also keep a collection of calendars, booklets, publicity material and mail order catalogues.

Now that I have this image bank, I can quickly put together displays like the ones shown here without wasting hours of my time dredging up suitable pictures. As with all banks, if you make sure you don't take more out than you put in, you'll find it pays you with interest, this time the classroom variety. Once the rest of the world knows what you are doing, then you will find that they begin to divert interesting things your way, giving you a steady supply of new pictures and a waste bin which is worth emptying!

The display pictured on this page came about after a school visit to the zoo. It took over the whole primary school. The visit iteslf stimulated a huge outpouring of related work, a zoo after all embraces geography, science, the visual arts, to name but three, but see how the display has acted as a focus for the activity.

You will find that when a child is working on something that will subsequently be displayed, not only will the work be of a higher standard but sometimes, you could be forgiven for not recognising whose work it is — it's so good! A proper display has this exciting positive feedback effect. One of the aims of this book is to demonstrate the wealth of available techniques that will enable you to make your own stunning displays.

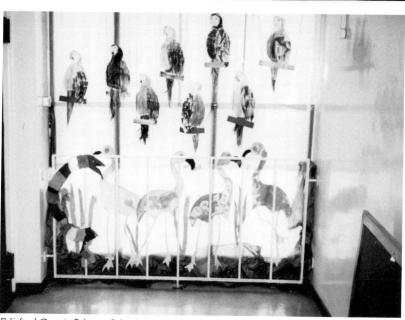

Edisford County Primary School

In this introduction, I hope I have persuaded you of the importance of display skills. You will find this book divided into two parts: in the first, I will look at the basic elements of classroom display. But please don't take my word as gospel! All my suggestions are tried and tested, but there are only 24 hours in the day, so I don't claim to have discovered everything! And if I say something can't be done, take it as a challenge. Even if you don't prove me wrong, you may discover new effects and techniques in the process. The second half of the book looks at 'display skills' writ large: how to make booklets, mount exhibitions, and apply your display skills to enhance the reputation and image of your school.

Edisford County Primary School

MAKING USE OF SPACE

The essence of effective display is the control of space. Our aim is to catch the eye, and to give it time to absorb the information present. We do this by balancing busy areas against restful ones, and offsetting areas of calm with areas of animation. In addition, there should usually be a sense of direction within the display which guides the eye from one area to the next. The obvious answer here is arrows and numbers, but you will find, as often as not, that if you can lend to your display an inner cohesion, so that each unit looks as if it belongs just where it is situated, these clumsy pointers won't be needed. This is far more elegant and satisfying. Without this underlying logic, the message of a display will be lost behind a buzz of background noise.

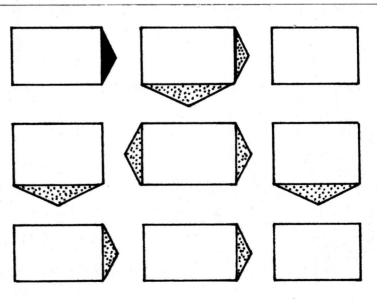

There are countless strategies which you can employ to unify even the most discordant shapes and colours.

Achieving Coherence from Variety

Many designs have a sense of direction which you should be aware of (see right). This property should be harnessed unobtrusively, so that the viewer's eyes come to rest within the sheet, rather than outside it.

Look at these methods of linking items together:

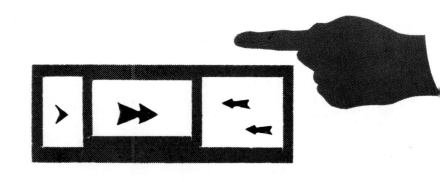

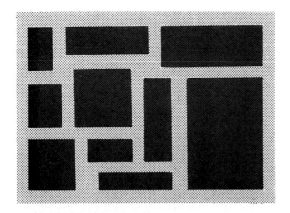

A common border but no direct edge-to-edge pathway.

A more relaxed arrangement using foundation stones only

Dual axes giving internal unity.

If you have the space, lay the boards flat so you can test a number of variations.

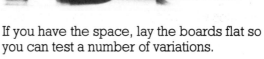

The central axis. This is particularly good for long panels.

Headlines and titles need space — sometimes lots of it. Below, you can see what you can do with an uncluttered image and a brief title.

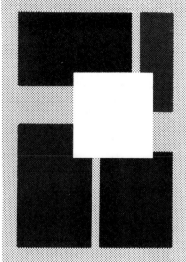

Here, you could put a section of text or a banner headline in the white area to draw attention to the pictures.

Scale is important. Here the large main images are supported by the smaller units which supply detailed information in pictorial form.

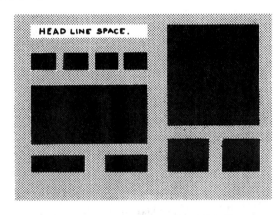

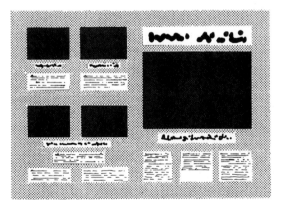

Aim to achieve balance. Note the effect of this display: the first thing we notice is the main title, and the principal picture. Then the lesser images call our attention, and their captions should put them into their overall context. And if we find we are interested in the subject matter, there is a more detailed piece of text at the bottom which we can read at our leisure.

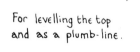

For levelling the top and as a plumb-line.

There's no need for you to wrestle for hours with a protractor when setting up. Let gravity come to your aid. I always use the 'scissors and string' method that's pictured. And when it comes to ensuring that you have regular borders and spaces, a piece of specially cut card works a treat (folding it makes it easier to hold).

Dealing with identically shaped images.

A neatly ordered array of squares is always a safe bet — nothing can really go wrong — but it is rather dull and does nothing to the material except leave it alone.

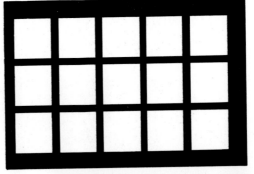

But the moment you start experimenting the fun begins. This arrangement might be suitable for a collection of poems written by children after a visit to a local factory perhaps.

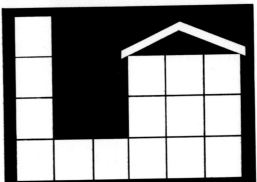

How might we present a collection of mouse poems? Here are some possible, yet simple solutions. If you have a class of potential poet laureates, perhaps you could set a general topic — i.e. animal poems, and let the children cut out animal shapes and then write suitable poems to fit them.

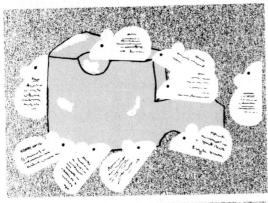

Edisford County Primary School

A very large display can be one of the most enjoyable types for all concerned. Each child has his own responsiblity, ranging from adding his own bit of tissue paper or whatever, to being in charge of a whole section of the display.

Rishton Methodist Primary School

Brookside Primary School

Stencils could perhaps provide each child with a basic shape to use. And what about some simple printing methods? Things like inking up real leaves, or making card and potato shapes, are within the scope of even the youngest children.

This can be extended to three dimensions with groups collaborating in making members of a clay village or contributing players for an orchestra of clay musicians.

Edisford Primary School

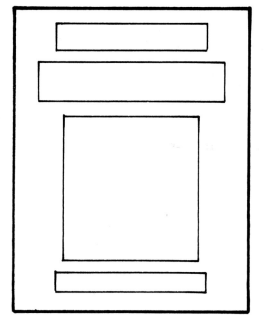

Balance, diagonals and overlaps

Unassuming, peaceful, symmetrical arrangements like this one are again safe but dull. It has a classical feel to it (you can almost smell the olives) but what worked for the Parthenon won't necessarily work for you. And in any case, this shape doesn't quite work. Try covering the bottom black line and you will see how the shape relaxes. This suggests to me that too little space was originally allowed there. If you try to use this shape for poster work, you will encounter similar difficulties, because you have to judge things like letter size very finely indeed.

This is a much more lively composition. The strong diagonal, and the conterbalance of the stepped and bottom blocks gives it a much more vital effect. Allowing the diagonal to 'bleed' off the page makes the whole thing stand forward more boldly.

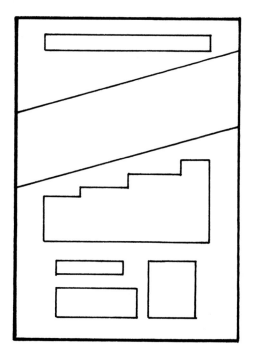

The montage of seated fashion models below shows diagonals in action. See how it makes us look carefully at human proportions.

This engineering design sheet uses a number of these methods. The bold and slightly offset title block combined with the large graphic image, the design and stages in the manufacturing process, all in all create a very pleasing balance.

Work can be enhanced enormously if suitable borders are used. These borders may be no more than margins, or at the other extreme, complex decorations and designs in their own right. But they must be chosen with care. The colour of the backing paper affects the way we look at the picture. If you want to draw attention to the reds in the piece, use red backing paper, a blue paper for blue etc. A dull piece of work can be 'jazzed up' by using a combination of colours.

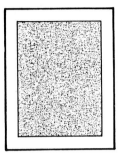
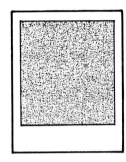
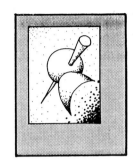

Balance is crucial. The uniformly even border on the left is not nearly so interesting as the one in the centre. See how a border can counterbalance an unbalanced illustration like the one on the right.

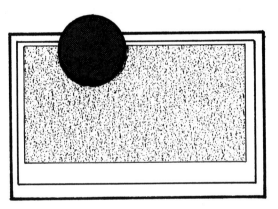

Borders may be broken to attract attention generally, or to focus on a specific point.

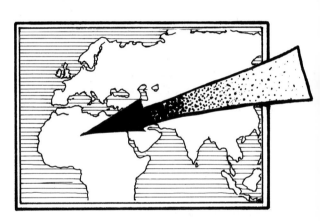

Sometimes the illustration or print includes its own plain margins.

However, work can also be trimmed and surface mounted onto a suitable colour . . .

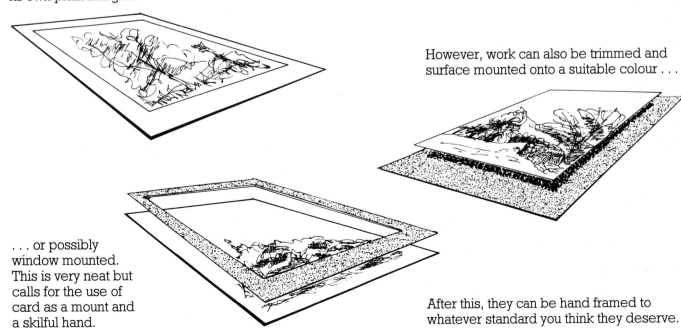

. . . or possibly window mounted. This is very neat but calls for the use of card as a mount and a skilful hand.

After this, they can be hand framed to whatever standard you think they deserve.

I mentioned complex borders earlier. You could do these by hand of course, but why not have a look through some resource books which are full of copyright-free material? These 'Instant Art' borders, corners and friezes are there for the picking.

You may be as complex or as simple as you wish. A modest corner piece may well achieve more than this lush extravaganza below.

Many different designs are available.

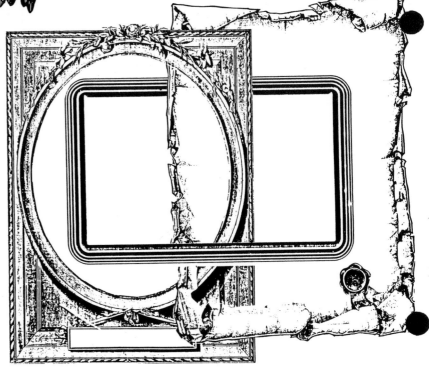

These ideas may be copied, traced or photocopied to add a new measure of interest. They may be the starting point for a sensitive piece of work.

If you have access to a photocopier with coloured inks, all the better.

CAUTION THIS CAN BE ADDICTIVE!

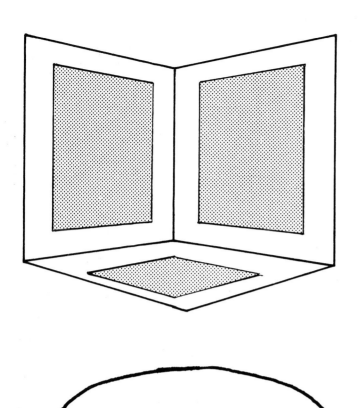

Using three-dimensional space

After worrying about balancing diagonals for hours upon end, it's easy to forget that human beings are three-dimensional creatures. The same is true of displays. Be on the lookout for ways in which you can utilise all three dimensions. I think that there are four main classifications of display space. 1. The flat wall. 2. The simple corner. 3. The 'window' space which has a definite front and is bounded at the sides. 4. Open space around which the viewer can walk.

Is there any way you can expand into adjacent space?

With a few bricks and heavy duty cardboard tubes on your side, you can easily construct robust display furniture which will last for some time. Get out your paint and see what you can do. With a little effort, even tiered pedestals should be within your grasp. And anything will do to prop up a flat piece of work.

If you have the luxury of space, use it!

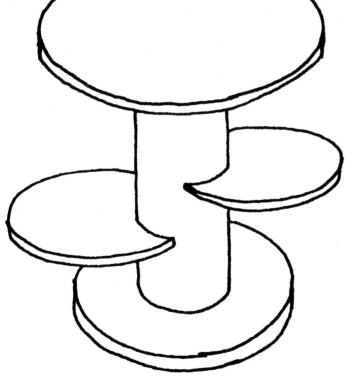

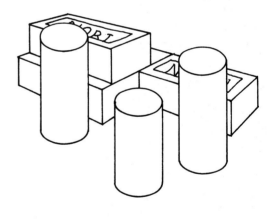

Nothing catches the human eye more quickly than movement. Have you ever thought of using mobiles as display equipment? They can be very attractive. You can usually rely on draughts to keep them moving, but if not, a light bulb will cause enough air turbulence for some purposes. And don't forget electric fans and power turntables. Can you get your hands on any of these? Might there be a spare one at a Teachers' centre?

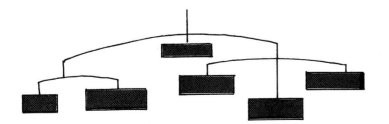

21

Ideas for three-dimensional displays

These displays invite the viewer to interact in sometimes quite sophisticated ways. As he walks around he may witness all the units he has just been looking at meaningfully change their relationships with each other as he reaches a new perspective. This gives the imaginative exhibitor tremendous scope. Most displays are too delicate to encourage physical interaction, but where possible, this should be encouraged. A really good exhibition is difficult to leave alone.

The display on the right makes good use of pupil involvement and space.

Edisford Primary School

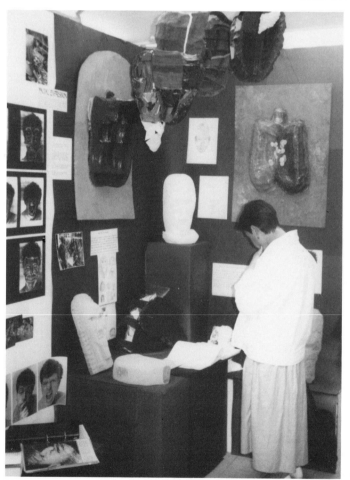

Didsbury College of Higher Education

Primet High School

Here, the mature student has learned from her geology lessons. She has made good use of her corner by arranging some of her materials into 'stalagmites' and 'stalactites'.

This art assessment is a personal favourite. See how she has made imaginative use of the cascade from the top right, and of the middle space by her placing of hanging baskets. A joy to mark!

MATERIAL AND METHODS

In this chapter we shall look at the various raw materials you will need, and some simple equipment which you will find useful. Let us start with the most basic.

Paper, card and board

Whatever the exhibition or display, it is certain that paper, card and board will feature in it somewhere. There are so many different kinds, thicknesses and qualities that it would be possible to write a book on this subject alone. As a teacher who is interested in display skills, the knack is to maintain a good stock of different types so that you can find just what you want for any occasion. Paper is almost a capital investment because it does not go off, stores economically and you will be sure to find a use for it some day. If any of your yearly allocation is left over, and such things have been known to happen, then think about buying paper.

Better still, think about acquiring paper without paying for it. Legally that is! It is remarkable how much perfectly usable paper is thrown away every day by industry. This may be a waste product from some luxuriant manufacturing process, but it is more likely to be from your local printer. They often have off-cuts, reject sheets printed on one side or small surplus quantities of an unusual size or colour. Unbelievable as it may seem, they may have to pay to have it taken away. If you ask, they may give it to you instead. Many people hate to see waste and are only too willing to give it to a good cause like your school. Make tactful enquiries and you may be pleasantly surprised at what you are given. Another surprising source of paper can be the stockroom of your own school. Perhaps some other department ordered a supply which proved unsuitable for the purpose and has since been forgotten. There may be several packets which are yours for the asking.

If you have money to spend, you'll often find that L.E.A. contractors prove much cheaper than commercial suppliers. Try to avoid buying odd sheets of card at local shops as prices can be really quite silly. If you become completely intoxicated with paper and can visit the Covent Garden area of London, then you will find a number of specialist shops there which have the most wonderful range of textures, thicknesses and colours.

Paper makers?

Paper suppliers?

Metric paper sizes

The most basic size for paper is AO which has an area of exactly 1m². It is rectangular and the edges are in the proportions of 1 : 1.414. This means that sheets of 'A' size can be cut in half and still remain in the same proportion. For instance, A1 is exactly half of AO, A2 is half of A1 and so on. This book is of size A4.

The diagram shows the relationship between the A sizes from AO to A6, and gives their measurements in mm.

Note that each corresponding length is 71% of the next larger size. Since printers need to be able to fold the paper and then trim down to the A sizes, paper is sold also in two ranges called RA and SRA. The measurements are given here.

A2 420 x 594		A1 594 x 841
A4 210 x 297	A3 297 x 420	
A5 / 148 x 210	A6 / 105 x 148	

The 'B' series is an alternative range of paper sizes which is less widely used. The proportions are still 1 : 1.414 and a half sheet still has the same shape as a full sheet. An 'A' size is 84% of the corresponding 'B' size.

The 'C' sizes are mainly used for envelopes and allow a little space all round so that 'A' size letters and brochures can be inserted. For instance an A5 leaflet will fit comfortably into a C5 envelope. The A4 size is most commonly used for letters and simple leaflets. Folded in half it will fit into a C5 envelope. Folded into three, it will fit into a DL envelope.

millimetres		*millimetres*	
RA3	305 x 430	SRA3	320 x 450
RA2	430 x 610	SRA2	450 x 640
RA1	610 x 860	SRA1	640 x 900
RA0	860 x 1220	SRA0	900 x 1280

A Series

	millimetres	*inches*
A7	74 x 105	$2^{15}/_{16}$ x $4^{1}/_{8}$
A6	105 x 148	$4^{1}/_{8}$ x $5^{13}/_{16}$
A5	148 x 210	$5^{13}/_{16}$ x $8^{1}/_{4}$
A4	210 x 297	$8^{1}/_{4}$ x $11^{3}/_{4}$
A3	297 x 420	$11^{3}/_{4}$ x $16^{1}/_{2}$
A2	420 x 594	$16^{1}/_{2}$ x $23^{3}/_{8}$
A1	594 x 841	$23^{3}/_{8}$ x $33^{1}/_{16}$
A0	841 x 1189	$33^{1}/_{16}$ x $46^{13}/_{16}$

B Series

	millimetres	*inches*
B5	176 x 250	$6^{15}/_{16}$ x $9^{7}/_{8}$
B4	250 x 353	$9^{7}/_{8}$ x $13^{15}/_{16}$
B3	353 x 500	$13^{15}/_{16}$ x $19^{11}/_{16}$
B2	500 x 707	$19^{11}/_{16}$ x $27^{13}/_{16}$
B1	707 x 1000	$27^{13}/_{16}$ x $39^{3}/_{8}$
B0	1000 x 1414	$39^{3}/_{8}$ x $55^{11}/_{16}$

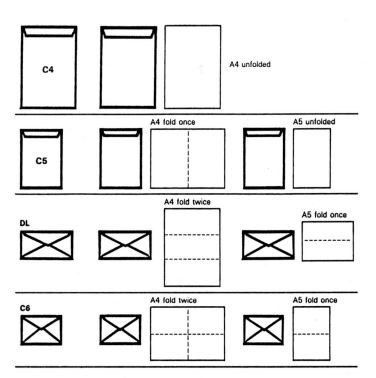

Envelope C Sizes

	millimetres	*inches*
DL	110 x 220	$4^{5}/_{16}$ x $8^{5}/_{8}$
C6	114 x 162	$4^{1}/_{2}$ x $6^{3}/_{8}$
C5	162 x 229	$6^{3}/_{8}$ x 9
C4	229 x 324	9 x $12^{3}/_{4}$

Other paper sizes

Sugar paper size	505 x 635 mm
Double crown	508 x 762 mm
Octavo demy	216 x 138 mm
Octavo royal	234 x 156 mm
American quarto	216 x 279 mm
Computer paper	216 x 279 mm

Paper weights and thicknesses

The weight of 1 square metre of paper in grammes is written as G.S.M or g/m² and this is the commonest measure of paper weight which is used today. The higher the G.S.M or 'grammage', the heavier the paper, but there is not a direct and absolute correlation between the weight and thickness. The thickness is measured in 'microns' (thousandths of a mm) or in 'thou' (thousandths of an inch). Depending on the type of pulp used, the surface coating and the amount of rolling during manufacture, the 'bulk' or 'gauge' of the paper can vary considerably within papers of the same 'grammage'.

Card in 'sheets'

You may also see card referred to in 'sheets'. For instance it is still common to refer to '2 sheet manilla' or '4 sheet card'. In some senses this is a relic from the pre-metric past, but it may be helpful to have a rough conversion into microns. The figures are approximate and you will find that different conversions are given by different sources and from different manufacturers.

Paper quantities

One quire = 25 sheets
One ream = 500 sheets

The imperial equivalents of 24 and 480 sheets are now scarcely ever used.

Paper/Board Gauge Conversion Table

micron	thou	micron	thou
25	1	280	11
35	1½	300	12
75	3	380	15
125	5	430	17
180	7	500	20
200	8	580	23
230	9	750	30
250	10	1000	40

The thickness of a sheet of paper or card can be measured with a micrometer if you take care not to indent the surface.

sheet	micron
2	600
3	900
4	1200

Other paper qualities

Opacity

This determines how characters or images on one side of the sheet show through from the other. High opacity is usually desirable.

Absorbence

The surface quality of the paper determines how well a paper absorbs ink or paint and therefore how intense an image can be obtained.

Texture

The surface of the paper can be altered by the treatment it receives during manufacture. It can be made to be smooth, medium smooth or rough. Sometimes a paper with a rough surface is said to have 'plenty of tooth'. Such paper accepts pencil or charcoal very well,

The right material for the job

The paper industry invests millions of pounds each year in research and development of new products and it is worth writing for samples. They are usually very helpful and it will keep you in touch with new ideas. You can test samples for their suitability for your own actual needs. Try exposing the samples to sunlight for an extended period (if you live in England, you may have to skip this bit!) and see if they fade. See what happens when the sample gets wet. How well does it cut or fold? Will it withstand the scrubbing of an eraser, or a vigorous painter? Will it take felt tip or pen? The table below gives some commonly available types of paper.

PAPER TYPES AND QUALITIES

Product	GSM	Microns	Comments
Layout paper	60	80	Smooth, translucent, cheap, and tough. Allows images to be overlayed to check composition.
Light technical cartridge	60	80	Open textured, opaque, very absorbent, good cheap practice paper. Yellows quickly on exposure to light.
Newsprint	60	80	As above
Tracing paper	63 and 90		Very smooth, highly translucent, very tough, resists abrasion well. Several layers can be built up on top of each other. Good for technical work.
Duplicating paper	70	120	Smooth, opaque, cheap and tough, very absorbent. Store dry. Different colours allow colour coding for covers and discrete sections in a book.
Photo-copying paper	80	120	Quite smooth, opaque, cheap and tough, highly sensitive to damp. Has a rather abrasive surface — wears out pens.
Poster paper	90	120	Usually matt finished, opaque and tough. Excellent fade resistance.
Cartridge papers	90	150	Good practice paper. Various surface finishes, opaque, surface usually disintegrates under a scrubbing action.
	100	185	Everyday art paper, opaque, surface usually disintegrates under a scrubbing action.
	130	225	Exam level art paper, opaque, surface usually disintegrates under a scrubbing action.
Sugar papers		240	Rough texture, highly opaque, tough, good for pastel work and charcoal. Most coloured sugar papers fade quickly.
		300	Ditto but good for mounting.
Manilla card		600	Smooth, tough. Similar in thickness, durability and structure to most cereal packets. Good for folders book jackets and models.
Boards		1,000	Heavy enough for surface mounting work. Boards are often coloured on one side only. Very large range available.
		1,250	Good for large surface mounts and small window mounts.
		1,900	At nearly 2mm thick this is good for larger window mounts. There are thicker boards than this.
Strawboard		1-2,000	Good for flat work or cut and taped models, breaks up on folds. Good for bookbinding.
High impact polystyrene		250-6,000	Very smooth and stable, resists damp. Excellent for draughting work with technical pens and model making. Unsuitable for water paints.
Corrugated card			As used in making cardboard boxes, excellent for large structures.
Crepe paper			Hopeless when wet otherwise colour fast and very flexible.
Water colour paper			A wide range of qualities and weights, often rough textured. Withstands heavy use. Usually very expensive.

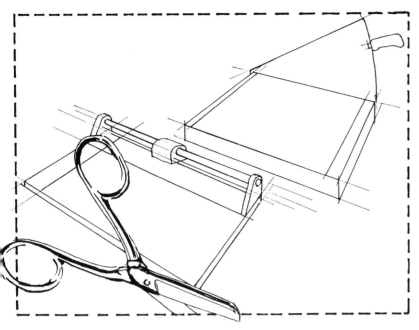

Cutting methods – Straight cuts

Scissors
These are fine for most 'cut and stick' jobs. The cheaper 'cold-cast' ones are good enough for class use, but I keep a pair of really good long scissors in my desk drawer for precision cutting and fabric use.

Rotary Trimmers
These are safe and easy to use. As long as they are treated well, they will give you good service. Their drawback is that they only accept small quantities of paper.

Guillotines
These aren't safe, and I wouldn't have one in my room. A guard may make them safer, but won't reduce their cumbersomeness or inclination to cut curves.

Straight Edges and Rulers
For accurate cutting, you need a good, steel, straight edge. To stop swivelling during a cut, put a small piece of plastic adhesive under each end of the ruler. The broad, bevelled edged types are best, especially if fitted with a finger guard. For classroom use the pressed steel safety rule is a good buy.

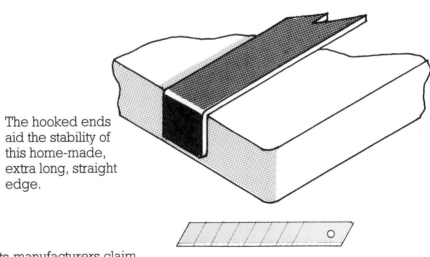

The hooked ends aid the stability of this home-made, extra long, straight edge.

Knives and Blades
The Stanley Knife really is as superb as its manufacturers claim. It also comes with a retractable safety blade, which is a bonus.

Look out for new products such as disposable knives and snap off blades. The old fashioned stiff backed razor blades are still available and some professional card cutters use them to this day.

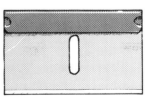

Cutting Mats
Usually a piece of scrap card or straw board will suffice, but you may want to buy a professional one. These have a printed grid on the surface and are 'self healing' i.e. the surface does not break up as you cut.

Be careful!
Craft knives can be regarded as offensive weapons in certain circumstances, so don't carry them in your pocket.

Cutting curves

Many graphic artists use a designer's scalpel for work. The blades are surgically sharp, easy to replace and there is a good range of shapes available. I have found that a curved blade is less inclined to drag on the surface of the paper. The tough little modeller's knife is good for senior work and the swivel blade next to it is superb for cutting round curved shapes. However, it is rather expensive for class use.

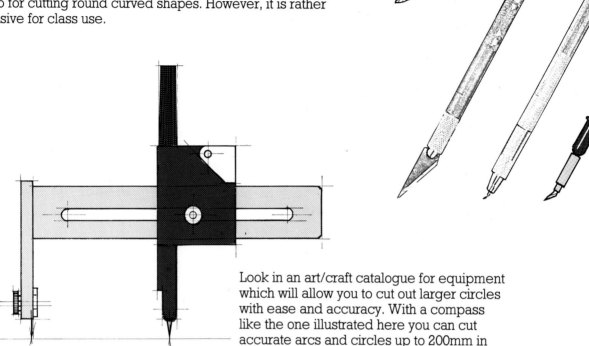

Look in an art/craft catalogue for equipment which will allow you to cut out larger circles with ease and accuracy. With a compass like the one illustrated here you can cut accurate arcs and circles up to 200mm in diameter.

Ellipses

These always look good but are difficult to cut. I often just cut around a stainless steel dish. You may also find a variety of oval dishes in the kitchen cupboard but be careful. Don't blame me if you then have to eat the Sunday joint off newspaper. More usually, you will have to cut freehand round a line constructed either geometrically or by pins and string.

To Construct an Ellipse

If you want to construct an ellipse of a particular size, here is one way.

1. Find the exact centre by drawing diagonals.
2. Mark major and minor axes.
3. Open compasses to radius xy.
4. Using this radius draw arcs from A & B to intersect major axis.
5. Put pins at intersection of arcs.
6. Make a loop of cotton or string around both the pins and the pencil point which should be A.
7. Follow maximum extension of loop left and right, top to bottom. The offcut can be used as a stencil or form to generate more ellipses of the same size.

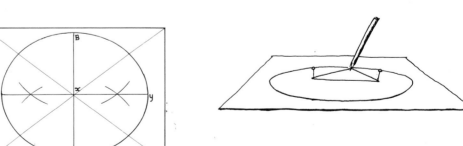

Cut a groove in the pencil point to guide the cotton.

Methods of fixing

Drawing pins

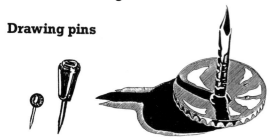

Staples

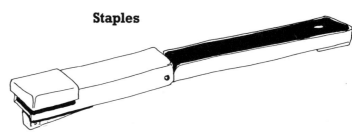

Drawing pins come in a large variety of sizes. They are cheap and reusable but the big drawback is their ugliness, which makes them unsuitable for important displays. Perversely, the smaller and more unobtrusive the pin, the easier it seems to go missing.

Check your catalogues regularly for alternatives. For displays, staples and special display pins are more suitable. Always pin through the darkest parts of the work where possible, and remember to use them obliquely. They are so much easier to remove that way.

If needs be you can open out a conventional stapler to use on display boards, but a staple gun is far more satisfactory. The one below looks very neat with its stow-away handle. When mounting work on chipboard, you really need a heavy duty staple gun. If you are prepared to sacrifice a little firmness, holding the gun obliquely makes it much easier to remove the staples later.

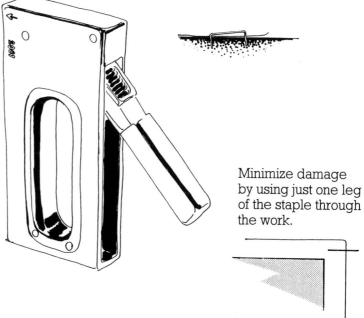

Beware of the rivet headed pins which can fail under pressure. Look for the solid dome headed pins instead.

Minimize damage by using just one leg of the staple through the work.

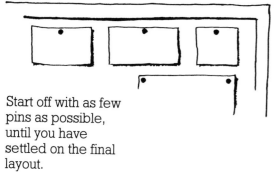

Start off with as few pins as possible, until you have settled on the final layout.

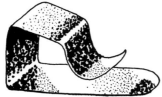

When it comes to removing pins, use a drawing board clip, not your nails.

At our school we make lots of these from mild steel as a craft exercise. They are very useful for removing staples and drawing pins.

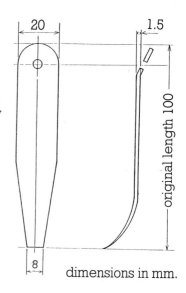

dimensions in mm.

Hanging heavy work

The standard picture hook, whether single or double, will hold a very heavy load when fixed to sound plaster, but if you are faced with bare bricks you may have problems. You can try driving in a masonry nail, but more likely you will have to drill and plug the wall first. There is nothing wrong with this, but it offers no flexibility. Think about putting up a picture rail. This old-fashioned method of hanging heavy work means that it is easy to adjust positions. Picture frames need stringing from side to side with durable cord which will not show when hung. Block mounts can be hung from a single nail if an absolutely central hole is drilled high up on the back.

Large floppy work may need extra support. Sometimes a plastic poster hanger or batten stapled across the top will suffice but for better effect a semi-circular section of wooden beading can be stained and attached.

Very temporary hanging.

Doubled over sheets can be used for drying work or temporarily storing it. They can be strung up high on wires across the room or parallel to a wall

Other methods

You can avoid using glue by any number of ways. Things ranging from paper clips to pop-rivets. Look out for big, fun-sized paper clips, magnets and velcro fasteners.

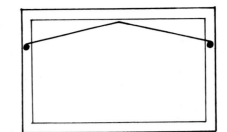

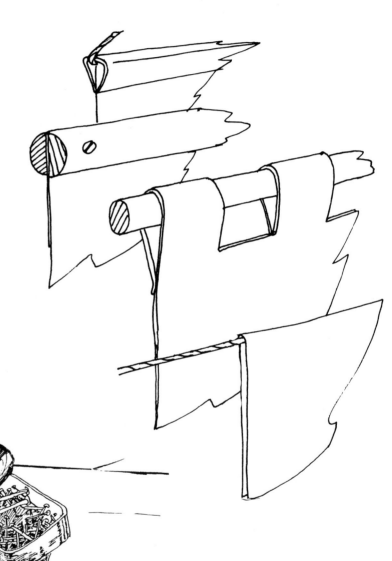

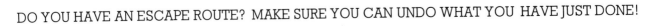

DO YOU HAVE AN ESCAPE ROUTE? MAKE SURE YOU CAN UNDO WHAT YOU HAVE JUST DONE!

Impromptu Shelves

The nature of a display may sometimes dictate that an item only 'looks right' at a particular point on the wall. If it is unsuitable for hanging you can save the day with an impromptu shelf. This one was designed by one of my students and made from a cereal packet.

If the touching surfaces are glued thoroughly and the unit staple-gunned to a suitable display board, it will bear up to around 2kg with safety.

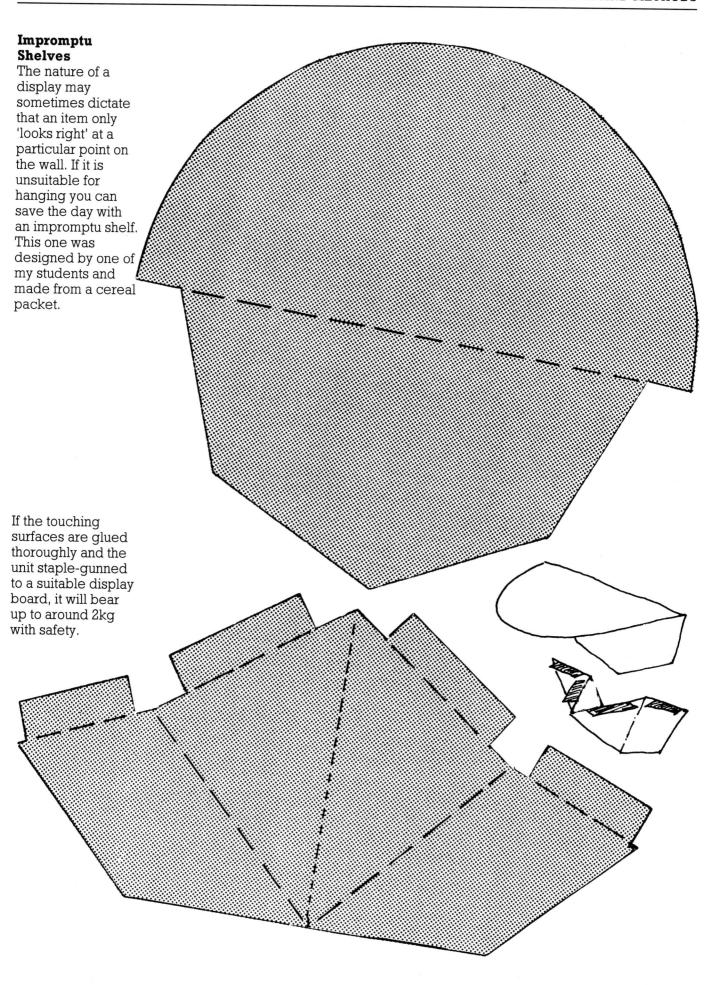

Picture framing

Protection

Picture framing is half aesthetics, half conservation. The piece in the photograph is next to an outside door. It needs protection from gusts of wind, and gusts of children. Ideally, it should have been behind a removable sheet of perspex, but this was prohibitively expensive. A cheap solution was to give it a covering of sticky-backed plastic. And the picture survives to this day.

Block Mounting

Block mounting is the cheapest method of permanent mounting. A chipboard or blockboard base has to be first cut to size, the edges must then be cleaned up, then bevelled, sanded and painted. I find that wallpaper paste is easily the most reliable adhesive. When block mounting it is customary to leave no border at all, allowing the picture to stretch right out to the edges of the baseboard.

Re-usable frames

The diagram below shows one way of making cheap re-usable frames which I discovered in a neighbourhood school. The frames were school-made, and were used for presenting photographs of school events, certificates and art work.

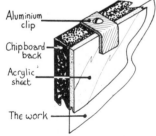

Aluminium clip

Chipboard back

Acrylic sheet

The work

Several firms market 'do-it-yourself' frames in a wide variety of shapes and sizes. You buy the pieces you want and have the glass or perspex cut to fit in the shop.

Professional Frames

For important material, the extra cost of a professional job is worth paying in the long term. A competent framer will advise on the frame, and use materials which are acid free.

Adhesives: the right glue for the job

Every adhesive has its uses. Rather than believe what the advertisements say, here is my own guide which you may find useful.

Plastic adhesives. For example 'blu-tac' and 'buddies'. These can bleed into the paper leaving oily stains. They can only bear a limited load, and are inclined to shear under as small a strain as 100g. Use a number of small pieces rather than big chunks. Remove the last little bits with a ball of adhesive.

Rubber solutions. For example 'Cowgum'. These are excellent for lay-out work as they grip firmly but remain tacky for a long time, allowing easy repositioning. Excess solution may be rolled off with the fingers when dry. Always replace the lid.

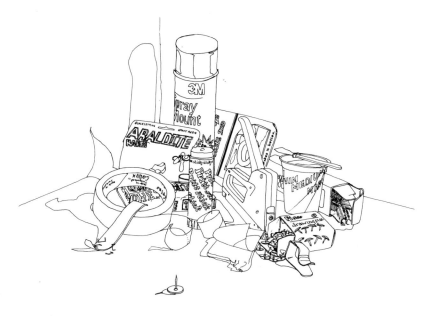

Cyanoacrylate adhesive. For example 'Super-glue'. This is banned in most schools because of its alarming ability to bond skin. The temptation to glue 'trouble-makers' into improbable shapes may be too much for a teacher to resist! It is superb for repairing fractured plastics, but needs a very smooth surface as it has no 'body'. Read the warning on the packet carefully.

Twin pack resin adhesives. For example 'Araldite'. Never be without this. It's excellent for serious bonding of most substances, is very tough, and long lasting.

Water-based glues. Powder paste is ideal for papier maché work.

Impact adhesives. For example 'UHU', 'Bostic' and many others. They are very useful as they will bond soft plastics and other non-porous substances. The very big drawback is that they are mainly solvent based and solvent abuse among the young is a terrible problem. Never stockpile them. Apart from the risk of theft, the products tend to degrade. All in all, you may feel happier not bothering.

SOLVENT ABUSE

Something we can do without

Cellulose pastes. For example 'Polycell' are best for large areas of paper sticking. Mix only as required unless fungicide is included in the powder.

Spray on adhesives. For example 'Photo-mount'. This is probably the best product available for mounting pictures and photos. Excellent for glueing down intricate cut-outs. Use plenty of scrap backing paper as it is difficult stuff to get off if it touches anything by accident. Some do weaken in time.

Solid adhesives. For example 'Pritt'. The lipstick type dispensers. The bond weakens after a while which is a problem. Remove any excess by rubbing with a (clean) finger. There are also solid glues in tubs. Both are economical in use, even though stick adhesives seem painfully expensive to buy. Neither product 'crinkles' the paper.

Adhesive tapes

Cellulose tape. For example 'Sellotape', 'Cellux'. Good for short term sticking (i.e. less than a year) The binder has a tendency to bleed into the paper.

Double sided tape. This is very useful for display work and a must for your repertoire.

Vinyl tape Heavy duty and waterproof, not really relevant to display.

Pads. Double sided self adhesive pads. Good for irregular surfaces.

Masking tape. Good for some graphics work.

Gumstrip. Water activated. Useful for all sorts of tasks. Tastes foul and puts you off your food. Cheaper than the Cambridge diet!

Hot melt glue. For example 'Bostik'. As used in electric glue guns. It's easy to get carried away, and you may regret it when you see the bill. Best used in spots for structural work.

Dry mounting tissue. This is a hot melt sheet of tissue which is placed between the work and the mount. The work is then ironed with a protective sheet of paper over it. This is a professional system. You would be better off with spray-on adhesives. Beware of air bubbles.

Always

Allow for paper expansion when treating large areas with a water based glue. Work outwards from the centre to avoid air bubbles when smoothing.
Use plenty of scrap paper under the pieces being glued and remember to renew it frequently, as this helps to keep the work clean. Most adhesives evaporate, so replace lids. Experiment on similar materials before tackling a special job.

LOW-TECH: HIGH-TAC
Double sided tape substitute.

Movable display boards

A good display board will last for years, so it's a good idea to shop around. Every time you go to an exhibition have a look at the boards you see in use. If you can, send away for details to the manufacturers. You might be able to get away with simple sheets of insulation board if you intend to use them only once or twice.

Special occasions, such as art exam assessments can often prove something of a headache. At my own school, we own several 8ft x 4ft sheets of pin board which are simply propped on window sills or tied to electricity trunking in front of windows. We lose natural light this way but gain hundreds of square feet of display space with the minimum of fuss. We take care to black out any sources of light which are liable to distract the viewer. The boards are 'dressed' flat on their backs before being positioned.

High quality pin board, chip board or even glass may be used with one of the most ingenious systems available. The 'Klem' Clamp system just holds two boards together at the angle of your choice. This is a minimal system which makes for flexibility. When used with good boards it is very durable.

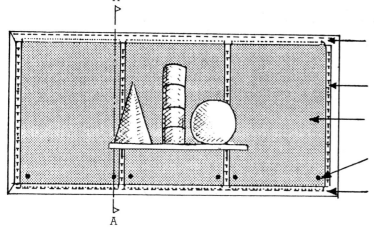

header space
boards slot behind upper frame

wall batten of adjustable shelving system

pin board lifts up into header space above and out over lower frame

finger hole to lift board out

board slots down into lower frame

section A-A

A framed display system, like the one illustrated here has many advantages. The boards lift out so that they can be dressed horizontally and the shelves can be moved and set up as required. The frame can be fixed to strong legs so that it is free-standing or it can be permanently fastened to a wall.

Portable display systems

Commercially produced display systems for instant display and 'carry away' use can be obtained, but I like this one of my colleague's which she charmingly calls a 'flannel graph'. Two sheets of corrugated card (the heavy duty variety used for packing fridges etc.) are covered with felt or some other cloth, which is then glued down at the back. Diagrams, pictures and text are pinned down with straight pins pushed in obliquely.

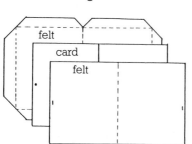

felt

card

felt

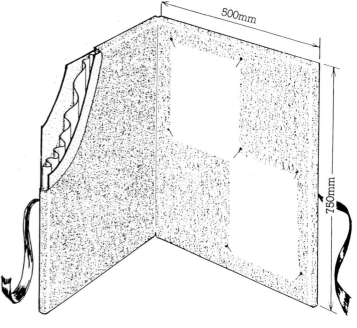

500mm

750mm

Buying display systems

Display screens

Screens and display boards are updated as often and with such ingenuity that anything I write about them will be out of date by the time my quarterly royalty cheque arrives. You just have to study catalogues, send off for details and make sure you are aware of the latest developments.

Before you rush out and spend your entire "Special Allocation" money on display screens, give a thought to the practicality of your investment.

Will you be able to lift it easily? It may look wonderful before your back goes but . . .

Will the boards withstand the rough and tumble of school life? Will it release plastic adhesives? Does it grip a pin? Will you be able to store it easily? Do you honestly have the room?

Display Cases

A good permanent display case is a long sighted investment. If it allows valuable and fragile objects to be exhibited with confidence, museums and parents may well loan you items which might not otherwise be forthcoming.

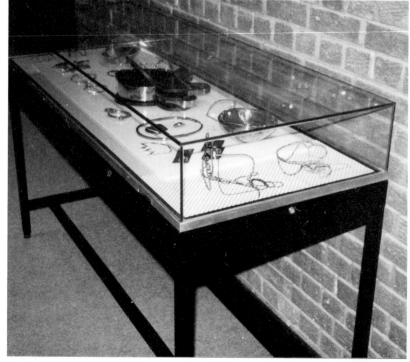

DEVELOPING IMAGES

Getting the most from school equipment.

In this chapter we shall look at the way common school equipment can be used for the enhancement of your displays. In my experience, too few teachers realise the full potential of the equipment which is often available in their schools.

The overhead projector

In daily classroom use, the O.H.P. enlarges images for all to see. This can be taken one step further. Some photocopiers accept transparent film, and this enables us to project maps, original artwork or photographs onto walls and large sheets of paper. Then these images can be made flesh, as it were, using paint or felt tip pens. If your photocopier doesn't do this, you can still trace the artwork onto the transparency manually. The enormous sizes of the images which can be produced can create a quite stunning effect. It is perhaps unwise to become too ambitious as the colleague of mine, who inspired the above illustration, found out. No sooner had he finished a heroic attempt to bring modern history to life on his classroom wall than technology took over. The computers arrived and he was banished to another room!

Using a zoom photocopier

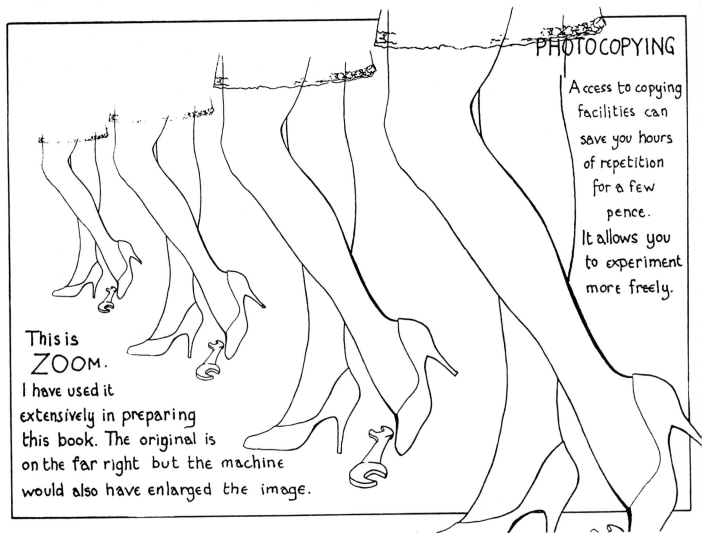

PHOTOCOPYING

Access to copying facilities can save you hours of repetition for a few pence. It allows you to experiment more freely.

This is ZOOM. I have used it extensively in preparing this book. The original is on the far right but the machine would also have enlarged the image.

Zoom copying is indispensable to the modern graphic designer. There are many copiers available which offer this facility. If you intend producing booklets, I don't see how you can begin without one. If you're unlucky enough not to have one, try your teachers' centre or the library. If all else fails, try commercial outlets, but if you do, be prepared to pay as much as seven times over the odds.

The most obvious use of the zoom facility is reduction on the grounds of economy. Two A4 sheets side by side can be reduced to a single A4 sheet with little loss of legibility. By careful use of reduction and an A3 'size for size' copier you can produce an eight page A5 booklet from a single sheet of A3. A booklet of this size can contain an impressive amount of information. Beware of distortion. Some machines are wonderful and you can do copy after copy and everything matches. Others allow 'creep' along one or more axes and with these machines you will have to be much less ambitious in what you attempt. Paper produced especially for copiers has a very low moisture content. If you are having trouble with distortion, check that the paper you are using hasn't become damp. The heat used to fuse the toner to the paper then causes it to buckle. For display, the enlarging facility can be used to blow up pages from home-made books or from children's work. The loss of sharpness does not matter if it is to be viewed from further away.

CAUTION
Not everyone loves fine print.

Calculating reductions and enlargements

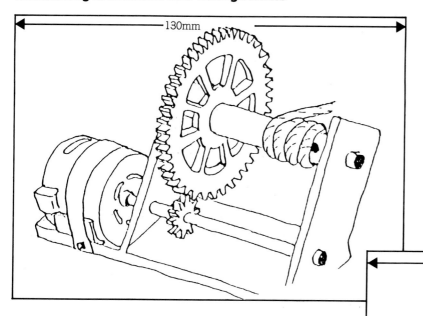

An enlargement or reduction keeps all corresponding lengths in the same proportion. To make an illustration fit into a certain space, you can use trial and error or calculate directly the percentage to set on the copier control panel.

$$\text{percentage} = \frac{\text{length on the copy}}{\text{length on the original}} \times \frac{100\%}{1}$$

If the answer is over 100, then it is an enlargement. If it is under 100, then it is a reduction!

We wish to fit the image into the frame.

To calculate the reduction needed
Measure the length of the original and of the required copy. In this case the length of the original is 130mm and we need it to be 94mm. The percentage is

$$\frac{94}{130} = 0.723 = 72\%$$

A true zoom photocopier will allow you to set this percentage. Others may only offer certain fixed percentages. In this case you would have to choose 71%

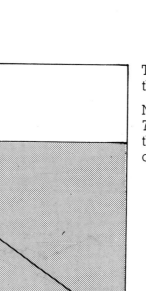

This diagram shows how an image remains the same shape after a reduction of 71%.

Note that the shaded area is not 71% but 71% of 71% which is 50%. Areas change by the square of the percentages shown on the copier control panel.

Standard reductions and enlargements

A3 – A4	71%	A4 – A3	141%
B4 – A4	82%	A4 – B4	122%

These are the standard settings you will see on many machines. The conversions between A4 and B4 are not precisely the same as on page 24, but it is close enough.

Retouching lines
After an enlargement or reduction the widths of lines are also changed in proportion and so any retouching must be done with a different sized pen. Fortunately the ISO (International Standards Organisation) sizes of technical pens are available in a wide variety of widths, making it easy to choose the correct one to use. For instance, a line drawn with 0.5 pen, and reduced to 71%, would need to be retouched with 0.35 pen.

Getting the best from the photocopier

The plain paper copier works best with clear, black lines. Large areas of solid black will seldom be printed evenly and soft greys are often less satisfactory still.

On the right is an example of what a copier will 'see'. The 7H pencil, 'liquid paper' (if spread evenly), grubby finger print and paper patch have all disappeared while the fine black pen-work and half-tone newspaper photograph have all copied well.

A copier will often ignore fine, hard pencil marks, so you may be able to leave construction and guide lines on the master sheet. But 'will often' and 'will' are poles apart, so don't assume anything. You just have to experiment. Printers write their instructions in pale blue on artwork or film and you may well find that your photocopier does not 'see' pale blue at all.

Photocopiers, like teachers, need rejuvenation from time to time. Regular servicing is essential.

Retouching photocopies An advantage of photocopying is that it allows additional work to be added without the risk of ruining what has already been completed. Corrections can be made by patching with clean, thin white paper, self adhesive labels or with correcting fluid. But be careful, some fluids dissolve photocopy print. However, there are correcting fluids specially formulated to avoid this problem.

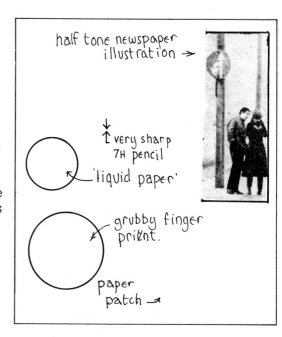

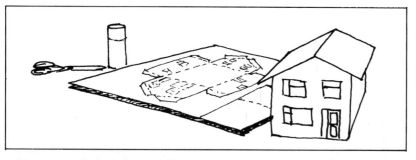

Copying on to thicker material

Most copiers will cope with thin card (2 sheet). This means that you can copy nets and outlines directly onto card, which is very useful when it comes to model or box making.

Copiers will also print onto acetate and other specially formulated transparent materials. Images like the ones illustrated here can give rise to moiré patterns. This is an interesting and fascinating subject.

On the left are small sections of the originals which were combined to generate these moiré patterns.

Making a mirror image

If you have a picture which is looking left and you want it to look right, then this is a simple matter to produce using a photocopier. First copy the image on to a transparent sheet. Turn it over and photocopy from it.

Yes, there is something strange about this pair of mirror images. The formula was written in afterwards!

Using a white dot screen

Photocopies of photographs or drawings with large areas of almost equal tone may lose detail in the reproduction. To help with this you can get a screen which has thousands of fine white dots on a transparent background. By dividing the image with smaller pieces, it often helps to maintain the definition.

A white dot screen seen against a pure black background.

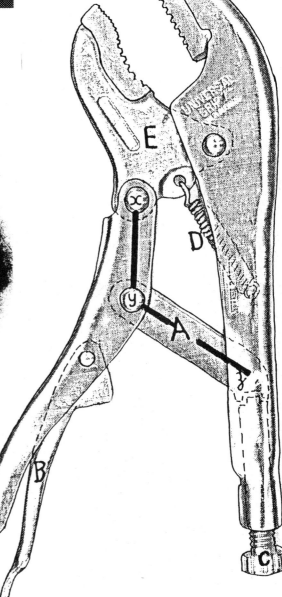

If the object is approximately flat, it can often copy surprisingly well. This mole grip would have taken a long time to draw, but it takes seconds to copy. If the result is unacceptably harsh then it can be softened using the white dot screen between the object (or photograph) and the copier glass. These two illustrations show 'before' and 'after' using the white dot screen. It also needed some retouching with a fine pen to restore the outline.

Instant Art: Copyright free material

A photocopier gives anyone who can put a coin in the slot, access to a mass of copyright-free material, which is available in specially collected books of images. These image banks are part of a rapidly expanding range which embrace all manner of topics from Archive art to Zoo pictures.

Repeated motifs

If you can use your copier to copy and recopy the same instant art motifs, then you can easily generate interesting borders and edging friezes.

ABCDEFGHIJKLMN

OPQRSTUVWXYZ

Double copying with instant art

You can generate some interesting images by printing an instant art 'network' background for your image. One method is to copy the network on to a transparent sheet first, and then position it carefully on your master before generating the final combined image. Alternatively, you can leave the final result more to chance by passing the paper through the copier twice, not forgetting to change the master!

Some of the networks which are available.

Here a home-made image is paired with an instant art cobweb. Try to use as many of your own images as possible, but don't hesitate to use instant art when you are in a hurry.

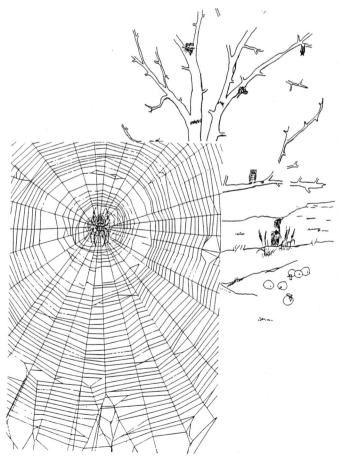

Computer graphics

The developments in this field are perhaps the most exciting innovations in our lifetimes. The resolution of the image on the screen is now far better than it was just a short while ago and further improvements may confidently be expected. Straight lines are getting straighter, curves are getting smoother! Colours are getting brighter and more easily achievable. It is not an exaggeration to say that anything you can reasonably imagine can be achieved by some method or other and that the cost may well be lower than you expect.

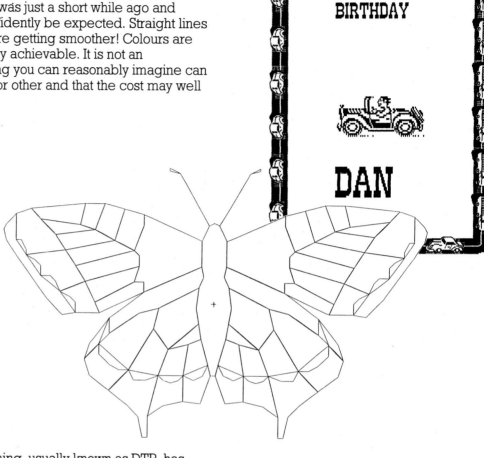

The advent of Desk Top Publishing, usually known as DTP, has revolutionised the integration of text and graphics in the production of printed material. Changes can be made instantly and electronically on screen and only when everything is satisfactory need it be printed out. The quality of the final print-out depends on the resolution of the printer which is available.

Graphic images can be generated by programming or by inputting drawings or photographs with a scanner. Once digitalised and stored within the computer the images can be manipulated at will and combined with other images and text.

You are unlikely to have the most up-to-date machines and programs in your school, but see if you can befriend someone who has access to both. I've yet to meet a computer buff who doesn't delight in showing off his machine and he may be happy to produce some artwork for you.

If you have no skill with computers yourself, try your students. These days, computer 'whizz kids' are legion and you can count yourself unlucky if you don't know at least one. Perhaps you could initiate a computer graphics project, such as designing a new letterhead, or tickets for the school play.

```
README
EPSON      PRN
IBMGRAPH   PRD
OLDELISH   LXM
OUTLINE    LXM
CYRILLIC   LXM
HEBREW     LXM
COURIER    LXH
BROADWAY   LXH
SHADOW     LXH
CYRILLIC   LXH
SCIENCE    LXH
EPSONFX    PRD
```

Dot matrix lettering can produce impressive results but, as you can see, they may be short of definition. But don't despair! Things are improving all the time. If you can obtain access to a laser printer, then you can produce results which are of publication standard.

These are some examples of the currently available typefaces, all of which can be expanded, condensed or slanted to give an almost infinite number of possibilities.

```
README
EPSON      PRN
IBMGRAPH   PRD
OLDELISH   LXM
OUTLINE    LXM
CYRILLIC   LXM
HEBREW     LXM
COURIER    LXH
B^C
```

```
README
EPSON      PRN
IBMGRAPH   PRD
OLDELISH   LXM
OUTLINE    LXM
CYRILLIC   LXM
HEBREW     LXM
COURIER    LXH
BROADWAY   LXH
SHADOW     LXH
CYRILLIC   LXH
SCIENCE    LXH
EPSONFX    PRD
```

```
README
EPSON      PRN
IBMGRAPH   PRD
OLDELISH   LXM
OUTLINE    LXM
CYRILLIC   LXM
HEBREW     LXM
COURIER    LXH
```

```
README
EPSON      PRN
IBMGRAPH   PRD
OLDELISH   LXM
OUTLINE    LXM
CYRILLIC   LXM
HEBREW     LXM
COURIER    LXH
BROADWAY   LXH
```

```
README
EPSON      PRN
IBMGRAPH   PRD
OLDELISH   LXM
OUTLINE    LXM
CYRILLIC   LXM
HEBREW     LXM
COURIER    LXH
BROADWAY   LXH
```

```
README
EPSON      PRN
IBMGRAPH   PRD
OLDELISH   LXM
OUTLINE    LXM
CYRILLIC   LXM
HEBREW     LXM
COURIER    LXH
BROADWAY   LXH
SHADOW     LXH
```

```
README
EPSON      PRN
IBMGRAPH   PRD
OLDELISH   LXM
OUTLINE    LXM
CYRILLIC   LXM
HEBREW     LXM
COURIER    LXH
BROADWAY   LXH
SHADOW     LXH
```

```
10 REM INTRODUCTION TO BEGIN PROGRAM
20 RANDOMIZE
30 PRINT CHR$(31)
40 PRINT "THIS GAME PROVE YOURSELF AGAINST THE GREAT DART PLAYER JOCKY WILSON"
60 FOR W=1 TO 6000
70 NEXT W
80 PRINT CHR$(31)
90 PRINT "IBM AND YOU HAVE JOCKY SUPPLEMENT SET"
```

Computers have problems too!

Photography

Photography has now developed to such a stage that you can obtain first rate results with the most basic equipment. The prints from even a very cheap camera are potentially good enough to be blown up to poster size. This is expensive, especially if you are using colour, but there are some excellent Do-It-Yourself kits for colour photography which may bring the costs down to manageable levels. For a geography exhibition, say, a full size poster photograph would be an attractive contrast to the usual proliferation of maps.

Photocopying photographs

Some photographs can be copied very well indeed. Curiously, the images obtained from colour prints are often better than those from black and white prints. There is a tendancy for the copier to clarify detail by sharpening the highlights, which you may find useful.

If the contrast is too harsh for your taste, try using a white dot screen again. It doesn't produce half tones but it does reduce the contrast a little.

Photographs from newspapers usually reproduce very well indeed. The image has already been 'screened' into 'dots'. Copyright may be a problem.

This picture is reproduced from a photocopy of a colour print

Lith Film

Without getting too involved in technical matters, it might be worth mentioning lith film. This makes obtaining forceful images much simpler. If you start with a good negative, this process produces a black and white print with no intermediate tones.

Such prints are excellent for wall displays, book jacket designs, etc. They can also be photocopied very faithfully.

Transparencies

We will all have used slides and projectors sometimes during our careers, but have you thought of using them in displays? A carousel projector can be left to run automatically as part of an exhibition. They can be used with screens or television sized daylight viewers, and linked to a soundtrack or commentary by means of an audio cue which the projector responds to.

Slides can be stored in clear wallets of twenty which are then kept in suspension filing units. This is a useful device as it makes them available to individual children.

A lightbox is not only useful for viewing slides. It is a great help in preparing graphic work with precise positioning. Backlighting helps accurate tracing.

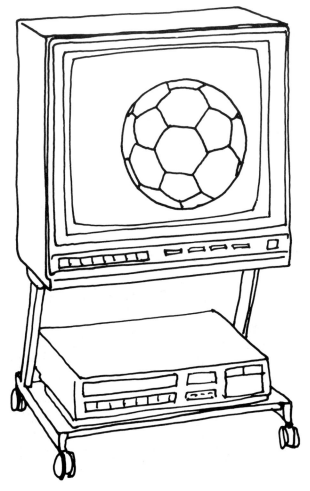

Video

Now that we are firmly ensconced in the video age, the recording of a unique school event is a very simple matter. Think how it used to be! Many schools now have a video camera which can give an almost instant playback, and the tape can be used and reused almost indefinitely. Incorporate this into your exhibitions. If you are doing a 'town' display, then in addition to artwork and photographs, you can show real film of the town. This puts the other exhibits squarely in their context.

If you don't possess this invaluable equipment, think about hiring for a special event. It's relatively inexpensive. Once again, try your Teachers' Centre first.

We have just been looking at ways of using school equipment. But let's now look at how we can use smaller, and often non-standard items.

Using a spray gun or airbrush

In the hands of a professional an airbrush can produce results of uncanny finesse, but at our modest level, we can use it most effectively for producing backgrounds.

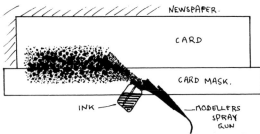

This is a very quick procedure. The card mask should be wiped down after each spraying to eliminate dribbles. The sharp line produced gives a good guideline for lettering or the edge of the picture. And to save setting it all up again, do plenty of 'back-up copies' in a variety of colours. Professional air brushes and compressors are prohibitively expensive. A cheaper alternative is a modeller's spray gun. The results are coarser, but not bad. A car's spare wheel will act as a reservoir, if you haven't a compressor and filling it can make an excellent detention!

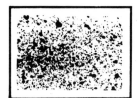

Tooth brush   Fixative spray

Low tech sprays

Even if you lack a mechanical spray, don't give up! A toothbrush and patience can give high quality results. The spatter is coarser, but can you use this to your advantage?

A finer spray can be obtained using an artist's fixative spray. All you need are a pair of strong lungs. The spray itself is very cheap and should be readily available.

Choosing the 'inks'

I usually use the Berol colour lab system of poster paints because they give consistent results, and offer an unsurpassed range of colours. To achieve a usable mix I add one part paint, to one part water, to one part air, and then SHAKE VERY WELL. If the paint is not mixed properly, you may have problems with the thicker blobs causing blockages. Other possible materials include Indian ink and the coloured aerosols used for retouching cars.

Making the masks

Masks can be thought of as either positive (stopping the spray) or negative (letting the spray through). In either case it is the contrast of the hard edge with the softer interior which gives spray work its special quality. There are three basic methods.

1. **Card cut-outs.** These are fastened onto the chosen spot with plastic adhesive.
2. **Transparent low-tac film** This is the best thing for fine detail. It can be replaced for reworking.
3. **Latex masking fluid** is applied with a brush and then rolled away after use. It is very suitable for schools, making it easy to produce neat, white lettering on a coloured background.

Producing complex images

Instead of thinking of a single mask and a single layer of spray, try building up the image in several stages. Masks can be partially removed or new masks added before the work is sprayed with a new layer or a new colour. The easiest masking material for this kind of work is transparent low-tac-film. It can be cut with a craft knife and then stripped away, ready for the next layer of spray. It can also be replaced after an area is sprayed with the first colour, so that it is not affected by a second or third colour. Then you might decide to replace only part of it so that some part is affected by either the second colour or the third colour or both!

Spraying is addictive and you will soon be fascinated by all the imaginative possibilites.

This splendid creature above was put together using spray and masking techniques. Indian ink was used and you will see that a few blobs have got through. However, they do not detract from the overall effect which is well within the scope of most schools.

The quality of the paper for such work is not too important, but you may find that the surface may strip off as you remove low-tac masking film. It is worth doing a trial to see if the material you have chosen wrinkles or distorts when wet.

Stages in the illustration above.
1. Pencil drawn rough work.
2. Pencil drawn shapes.
3. Pen dotted dragon.
4. All covered with low-tac masking film.
5. Outlines cut with craft-knife.
6. Landscape removed and sprayed.
7. Sky removed and lightly sprayed (including land).
8. Remaining film removed.

Repeated images — stencils

There are probably more stencils and templates available than you realise. Have a browse through any educational supplier's catalogue. Stencils are not only useful in their own right, but they can be adapted and improved with a little imagination. Stencils can make charts like these much easier to produce.

Making your own stencils.

The most suitable materials are card and thin plastic. The one below is made from 2.5 mm thick, 110 mm diameter piece of perspex. It took a little perseverence to make but was worth the effort.

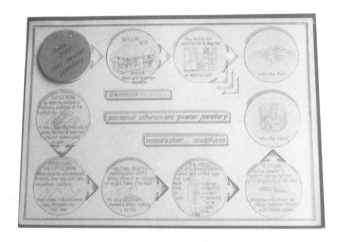

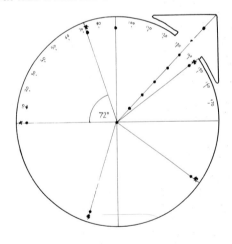

If you have no photocopier, stencils really come into their own for recreating exact repeats of both simple and complex shapes. Even if you have a photocopier, you will still find stencils most useful. You can place the images on a large background sheet wherever you wish and can change the colour and thickness of the outline at will.

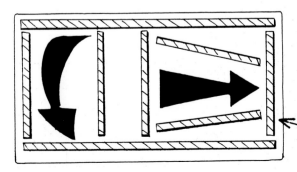

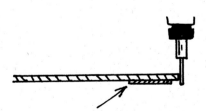

Remember the importance of an ink step to avoid blots.

Repeated images 'block printing'

Simple block prints are a very effective way to produce either borders or one-off prints. If you weren't looking for it, would you realise that the figure below is made from a repeating pattern? This will work with potato cuts, card, lino etc.

Tiny line logo blocks can be mounted on bits of wood or bobbins and used with an ink pad.

Enlargement

If you don't have access to a photocopier, or want to enlarge beyond the copier's normal scale, there are a number of manual methods you can use. Some are very old indeed, but they work, which is why they have survived.

Most people will be familiar with the pantograph, visually, if not in name. The arms are usually in the order of 300mm, but there is no reason why they should not be bigger. It is an imperfect method but it reproduces the general proportions quite adequately.

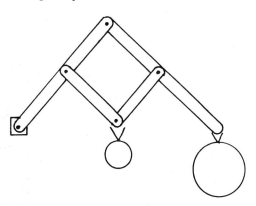

Squaring up is another well-known method. It can be rather tedious, but it is effective. The more squares you draw, the higher should be your fidelity. For variety, try multiplying the horizontal scale by a different factor from the vertical scale.

Children love to get their hands into paint and this is an excellent example of painting on glass by primary school children.

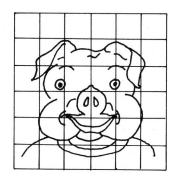

Using a stencil to create human forms

A simple stencil can be adapted to produce a number of related forms.

All of these characters are based on the form at the top of the page. The template has been turned as required, maintaining continuity.

Plus and minus a bit here and there, of course!

LETTERING SKILLS

Lettering is an immense subject with a history going back to antiquity. Many designers devote their whole careers to it like medieval monks, but sadly, many teachers find it all something of a chore. As I hope I shall show you, lettering can be fun, and when done with the right spirit, can perk up a display no end.

Good lettering can't be done in front of the television. You have to get yourself set up properly: you will need a well-lit bench at the appropriate height, and a board, sloping at a suitable angle. Even a pair of bricks will do! This will allow you to deal with the top of the sheet as easily as the bottom.

The calligrapher's check-list
Drawing board
Tee square
Hard sharp pencil
Rubber
Good long transparent ruler*
Set squares
Clips or plastic adhesive
Adhesive tape
Knife
Good ink
Pens
Brushes
Felt pens etc.
Stencils ·
Blotting paper
Plenty of good paper

*A ruler with both imperial and metric scales is preferable: you then have a wider choice of units which you can use for marking out.

Pens and markers

Felt tips are clean and always at hand.
Those with chisel-shaped tips offer the
greatest possibilities as they allow
maximum flexibility of line width. Try rolling
the pen whilst forming the letters — this
imparts a feeling of vitality into the script.

Spirit based markers will last longer than
water based ones, but they tend to soak
right through the paper which can be a
nuisance.

Check for colour permanence. Some
inks will vanish completely when exposed
to direct sunlight.

Look for the refillable varieties. And
always keep a close eye on your stock —
graffiti artists have light fingers.

ROLLING FELT PEN

SPIRIT BASED PENS BLEED INTO THE PAPER MAKE USE OF THIS

Pen Lettering

The only way to develop a feel for broad
and oblique nibs and what they can do is
through practice. Use one in a fountain pen,
and experiment (a technical term for
doodling!) whenever you can. There are
many types and styles of nib size, each of
which has its own characteristics and
problems.

tion from "manual" up to its
of "Craft, Design and Technolog
hing new in the individual parts

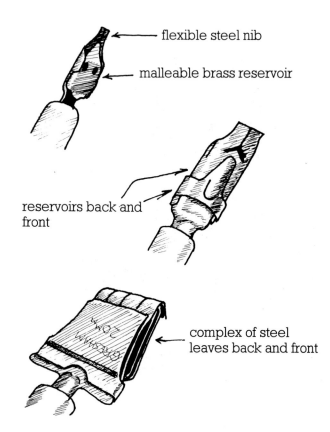

flexible steel nib

malleable brass reservoir

reservoirs back and
front

complex of steel
leaves back and front

best wishes

Don't be discouraged by your early
attempts. They are bound to be poor at
first. Fluency and confidence will come
eventually.

Brush lettering

The use of brushes to do lettering (which is what sign writers use) is something different again. Although the examples on this page have an obviously 'brushy' look to them, the 'best wishes' opposite was actually done with a brush. It has simply been reduced by our old friend 'Zoom.'

experiment

dry brush

new style

make it

happen

push your control
to the limits

TANG
TANG

simplify   adapt

fluid

Keep on experimenting! Once you have 'cracked' it, and gained confidence, you will soon start producing some really exuberant lettering.

SPRING
FEVER

Working on grids

A simple introduction to consistent lettering is to use these simple grids.

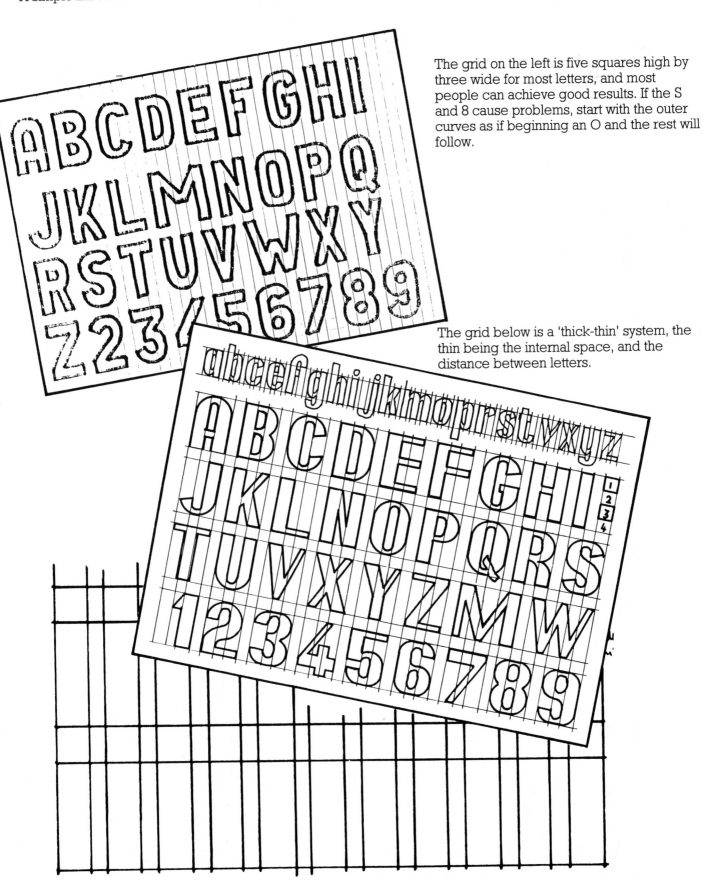

The grid on the left is five squares high by three wide for most letters, and most people can achieve good results. If the S and 8 cause problems, start with the outer curves as if beginning an O and the rest will follow.

The grid below is a 'thick-thin' system, the thin being the internal space, and the distance between letters.

Many papers are thin enough to allow a boldly drawn grid to show through, thus saving hours of marking up time.

3
4
3

and something more professional

Marking out

When you are dealing with a **simple** form, as pictured, draw guide lines at 3, 4, and 3 unit intervals with a very sharp, hard pencil. You shouldn't need to leave any space between these guidelines and the set immediately below it.

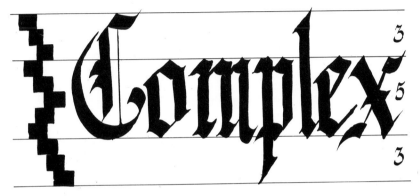

3
5
3

For more complex forms, I prefer to give the letters a little bit more space. As you can see, I have used 5 units accordingly.

Note that with some types of lettering, the 't' may be smaller than the other large letters.

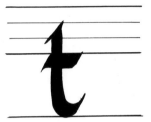

't is the runt of the litter.

sans serif

This simple direct sheet was produced to aid continuity during a long lettering job for a careers convention.

Illuminated capitals can be seductive !

57

Working with stencils

A little imagination can go a long way. Be free!

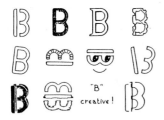

TILT4FUN
OVERLAP
BREAK
SHADOW

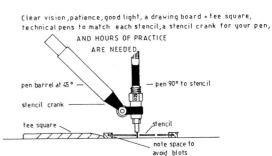

Professional stencils and a tee square can produce the most accurate results. But their creative applications are limited. Unless, of course, you know different!

°AⱭBCDEFGHIJKLMNOP₁RSTUVWXYZ   [(!?;:=÷+×˙ √°/₀8)]
°ᵃabcdefghijklmnopqrstuvwxyzₒ/1234567-°°9003

These stecils are very accurate, the wide range of sizes (some are tiny!) are copatible with photo copier enlargement and redution.

Sadly, stencils are all too often used with little or no imagination. So they become . . .

BORING.

Luckily, they can be adapted.

BRIDGE

Bridge the gaps to form real letters.

HATCH

Investigate textures and methods of colouring. Be thoughtful.

SERIFS

BURN

Take advantage of the fact that our brains often see more than our eyes.

Clear vision, patience, good light, a drawing board + tee square,
technical pens to match each stencil, a stencil crank for your pen,
AND HOURS OF PRACTICE
ARE NEEDED

pen barrel at 45° —   — pen 90° to stencil

stencil crank —

tee square —   — stencil

note space to
avoid blots

The ratio of line thickness to letter height is 1:10 in ISO lettering. (International Standards Organisation)

Stencils are like sirens, luring passing artists onto the rocks of carelessness. Don't use them when you are tired. The example on the left was produced at midnight, by, I'm sorry to say, me!

MAKE USE OF

SCALE

For BOLD headings

and general text

The stencilling above is done with the cheap flexible plastic type.

This block however is done with the professional rigid plastic type.

This is 'ISONORM'

These stencils are very accurate, the wide range of sizes is compatible with photocopier reduction and enlargement which makes for easier amendments.

Working from do-it-yourself templates

The template on the right can be made out of two sheet card, manilla or an old cereal packet. It has nearly all the lines and curves you need to draw the whole alphabet. Just move it up and down to place the section you need in the right place. With practice you will find it a very useful aid in setting out regularly sized letters quickly. All you need is a guide line.

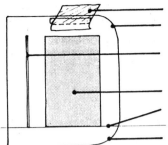

Sellotape tab to move template with

Curve from small coin

Slot for M & W and to set the spaces between letters

Basic letter size cut from card 3 units x 5 units

Line to follow guide lines

Curve from large coin

Of course, there is nothing sacrosanct about the exact proportions. The template below produces a script with an italic flavour.

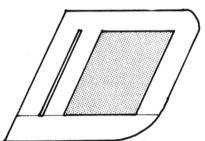

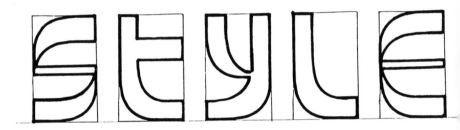

Once the basic letters are drawn and spaced out evenly, they can be modified and adapted to produce special script for a special occasion.

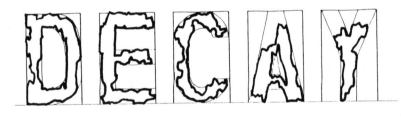

This runic curiosity looks like something that only Mr Spock could decipher. But actually, it is a perspex alphabet template, which I knocked up in a couple of hours. It shows what can be done. And it works. I like to edge each letter with a dark colour and fill in with something bright.

The ink step prevents bleeding under the stencil.

ABCDEFGHIJKLM
NOPQRSTUVWXYZ

This is one of my favourite templates which generates the entire alphabet. The curves are drawn using a pin and pencil. Try cutting a sheet of these letters out and then photocopying them against different backgrounds.

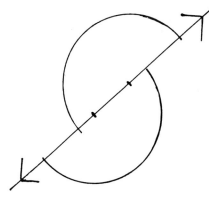

Experiment with the S
Start by marking the corners of the square, then draw the diagonal. Next use the 'S curve' pin hole twice (once for each curve) together with the pencil hole for large circles.

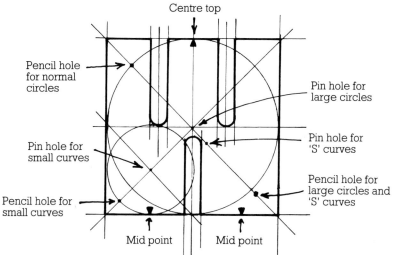

Centre top

Pencil hole for normal circles

Pin hole for large circles

Pin hole for 'S' curves

Pin hole for small curves

Pencil hole for large circles and 'S' curves

Pencil hole for small curves

Mid point

Mid point

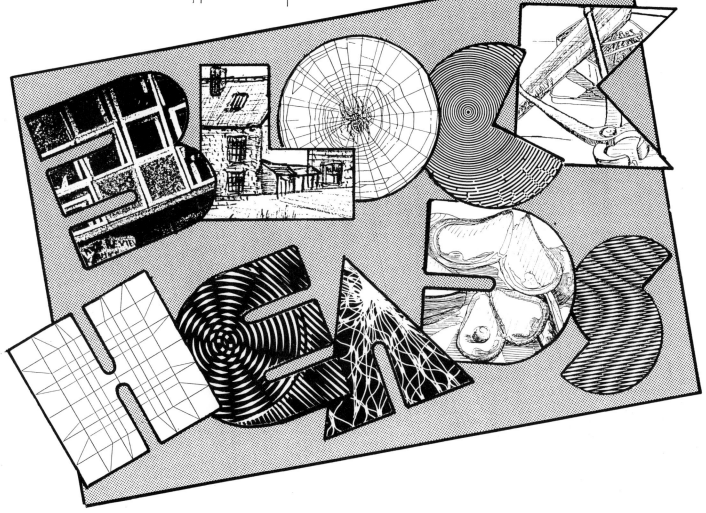

Letters with vitality

After looking at all these rather geometrical templates, let's see what happens if we ignore them. The letters in the picture below were torn — they weren't drawn out first. See how vivacious they seem.

All these letters are of approximately the same height because they were all torn, cut or hacked from a long strip of constant width.

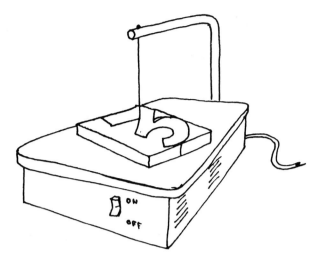

Three-dimensional lettering

As I noted earlier, we are three-dimensional animals, and this entitles us to three dimensional letters. Polystyrene is much the easiest medium to work in, whether you have access to a hot wire cutter or not.

If you can, cut several repeated letters together in one stack.

Avoid oil and cellulose based paints and adhesives — they eat into polystrene. Stick to P.V.A. if possible. Do ventilate well. And be especially cautious if using old packing case material. The fumes given off can be dangerous.

RAPID LABEL CO.

Dymo type

BLACKBURN AND DISTRICT SCOUT COUNCIL

Kroy lettering

Other systems

There are several machines available which punch out letters on adhesive tape. The best known is the 'Dymo' printer, which gives clear raised letters on tough plastic tape. This tape can survive the toughest possible conditions. The 'Kroy' printer comes with a good range of type faces, but its main purpose is to produce lettering suitable for photocopying. In addition, the letters tend to be rather fragile.

Look out for bigger and better versions!

Dry transfer lettering

There is a wealth of dry transfer lettering type-faces beyond the dreams of avarice. And not only in black and white. Letraset and Mecanorma are probably the two biggest names in the market. I would advise you to buy one of their catalogues, not just with a view to purchasing their products but for use as a visual aid. When used well, dry transfers are the best available method for achieving high quality lettering. It takes time to acquire the necessary skill, so don't be upset if your early efforts end in

failurè

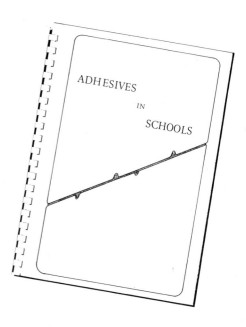

The catalogues, incidentally, give a number of hints on using these types of products.

England is now a multi-cultural society, and it is quite possible you teach children who know (or have parents who do) exotic alphabets and writing forms. Take advantage of this. Apart from promoting intercultural relations, it may stimulate you into developing novel letter forms. If this really interests you try adult education centres. Chinese lettering is a popular evening class activity.

If you can't find anyone with first hand information, there may be suitable books in a large library. Failing this, try the Citizens' Advice Bureau. They hand out helpful advice sheets, translated into as many as 7 different writing forms, which you can take home to study. But remember that C.A.B.s depend on contributions, so ALWAYS make a donation before you leave.

Copyright free

There are now many books of copyright-free material available.
Photocopy them several times, so that you have a supply of your
choice of lettering. What with the borders etc. which we looked at
earlier, you should be able to obtain professional results quickly
and with the utmost ease.

'Borrowing'

You are very unlikely to be sued for using cuttings on a non profit
making basis.

Can you steal the odd
word, or perhaps
parts of words from
newspapers?

When 'borrowing' from 'ordinary' material, make sure you know
the law, and never transgress the spirit of it.

Using calligraphy

Developing a complex and ornate style is all very well, but if you are faced with large amounts of lettering, you will need a minimal style which allows you to finish in hours, rather than months. So make sure you have a reliable second serve. Occasionally, for headings and other very short runs, you can come out with all guns blazing and indulge yourself. You might also consider keeping a good copy of these intricate letters shown below for your class. The children could embellish their history notes etc. by tracing or copying them.

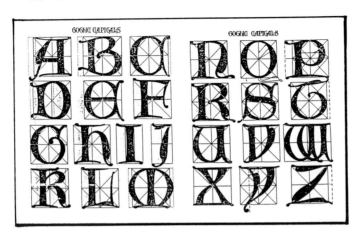

Some of the do's and don't's

Line space

DON'T DO THIS

UNDERLINING NEEDS SPACE

LETTERS NEED SPACE

THEN RUB THEM OUT

Word space

THERE IS NO
NEED TO BE
SHY

Generally speaking, if you have the space — use it.

THERE IS
NO NEED
TO BE
SHY

Letter space

Full, round letters need to be a little bit out-sized.

BDHIMNOQU ASTVWXYZ

Space-hogs share with nobody. Equal shares either way.

CEFGKLPR   J

Right wing sympathisers.   Just the one.

TU NI TJANTING TU NI

If one letter looks detached from the rest then it has too much space. Try to achieve a balance between the letters which contain natural spaces and those which do not.

Remember....

... and do look for a quiet corner to work in.

67

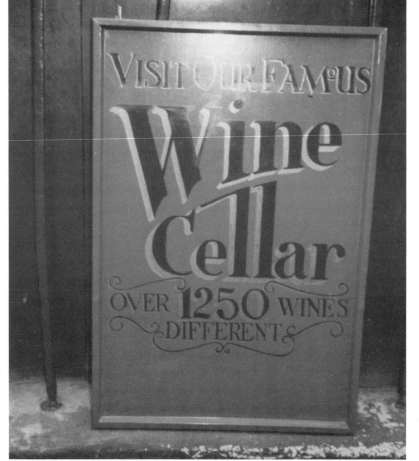

You are never too old to learn. See what the professionals do. The examples above were done by the wine merchant himself. He clearly has a respect for the formal values of lettering. Could this be your cue to restock your wine cellar?

Board displayed
outside D. Byrne & Co,
Clitheroe

PART TWO

CHAPTER 6

PRODUCING BOOKS AND BOOKLETS

MINERVA HIGH SCHOOL

NEW ENTRANTS
Notes for guidance

THE ALL WEATHER ART BOOK

SECOND EDITION

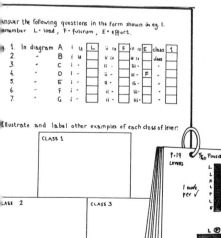

ESSENTIAL EQUIPMENT

You are expected to arrive prepared for lessons. Pack your bag the night before.

mm

1. A smile.
2. An apron.
3. A pencil, ruler, & compasses
4. Your **IDEAS**
5. Your homework.

deSign studies

design technology

STRUCTURES and MECHANISMS part 1

FROM THE DEPARTMENT OF DESIGN STUDIES. MCMLXXXVI

Answer the following questions in the form shown in eg. 1. Remember L = load, F = fulcrum, E = effort.

So far, we have been looking at the nuts and bolts of display skills. Now let's broaden our scope somewhat. In the next three chapters, we shall examine how we can apply display skills in a way that, apart from their intrinsic uses, gets them noticed. As I outlined in the Introduction, it is my firm belief that a school should do its utmost to promote itself as effectively and efficiently as possible.

In this chapter, we shall think about producing books and booklets. Look at the items pictured on this page. If a parent came across these on the kitchen table, or if one had been found left behind on the school bus, the reputation of your school could only benefit. Producing books, however modest, is something that most people, of whatever age, find irresistably exciting. Their enthusiasm is there to be harnessed!

What sort of book?

Before you start dreaming of the Booker Prize, let's make it clear what sort of books we are talking about. We mean collections of notes and fact sheets, booklets of scientific formulae etc. In these times of financial hardship, and the difficulty of finding suitable text books, there may simply not be enough books to go round. So when it comes to revision pupils must rely on their notebooks. This can be very unsatisfactory, because even the most eagle eyed marker will sometimes miss something important, leaving the notebooks as an unreliable source of information. This can be counteracted by the distribution of teacher-created 'fact-sheets' to be stuck in the notebooks where appropriate. Alternatively, you may prefer to put all these sheets into a single book which can be given or loaned to children as appropriate.

The book itself

This book is A4 size, but I favour A5 for school use. Notebooks tend to be A5 and by a form of natural selection, this seems to make them fittest to survive the school environment. A flimsy A4 book will be eroded by football boots etc. until eventually it has reached the optimum A5 size, doing wonders for theoretical biology but very little for its contents.

Ideally, like an armadillo, a school book should have a tough outer surface, but the obvious solution, a card cover, may well cause difficulties in the binding and printing process. If the book is to be given away, you will have to bind it in tough card, but if the notes are to be kept on the shelf for most of the time, then a paper front of a different colour will suffice.

Spring Bridge

Landscape.

Portrait.

Two basic formats

As far as I know there is no special reason to use one shape rather than the other. Yet I myself associate the landscape format with leisure and the portrait format with more serious factual reading.

What is artwork?

The artwork is the master copy from which your booklet is to be photocopied, duplicated or printed. It is usual to prepare artwork to the finished size if you are going to photocopy it, but to a larger size if you are going to print from it. The final reduction tends to hide many blemishes! For the kinds of booklets that we are talking about the artwork is likely to be a mixture of illustrations and text. 'Graphic Design' is the name which is given to the art of laying out the pages and good graphic design can make an enormous difference to success or failure in getting the message across. Traditionally artwork was pasted on to the thick and expensive boards, but nowadays this is not considered necessary. A backing of thin card or thick cartridge paper is quite sufficient.

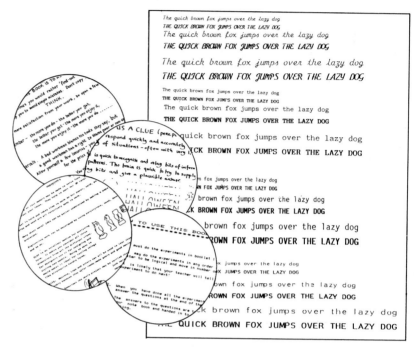

Producing the words

There are many possibilities. The text can be typed out on an ordinary manual or electric typewriter, using a carbon film ribbon if possible. It can be typed into a word-processor or computer, and then printed out on a printer. The three main types of printer are dot matrix, laser and daisy wheel, in increasing order of quality. The best quality of all is obtained from a typesetter and you have an almost infinite number of possible styles and sizes to choose from. It is also the most expensive method. It is a question of balancing the quality which can be obtained against the funds which are available.

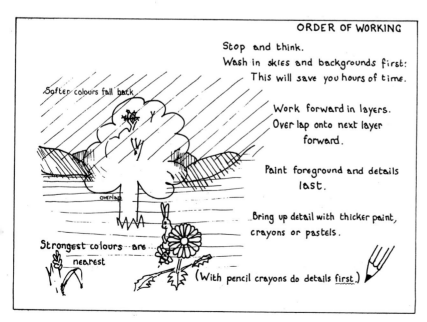

Last, but by no means least for school work, there is handwriting. As long as you use a black pen (and do not write like most doctors!) it will reproduce excellently. You can integrate text and illustrations very well and by its nature it encourages brevity and conciseness.

71

Reproducing the illustrations

The easiest type of illustration are drawings made with a pen only. The reproduction process is able to handle them directly and such work is known as 'line work'. If the illustrations are photographs or include tones obtained by shading, then they will have to be 'screened' first. This process divides the image into dots and allows the reproduction of a range of tones from black, through grey, to white. This screened image is called 'half-tone'. It will normally be necessary to go to a commercial printer to have your photographs converted to halftones. On a photocopier it is possible to improve the image of a photograph by using a white dot screen as described on page 41.

Adding tone to your work

As a way of avoiding the problems of half-tone, you can use a type of mechanical tone like 'Letratone'. With this you can make dramatic improvements to line drawings. It is simple to do and reproduces well, but test that the surface of your paper does not tear as you remove the excess film.

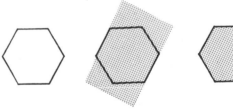

These tones are available in 10% steps and are graded by dot size. The percentage is the percentage of paper which is covered by ink. 0% tone is white and 100% tone is black. The various shades of grey come in between.

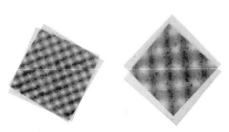

One tone pattern placed on top of another can give you moiré patterns. Experiment.

To use it, you cover the area and then trim to size. The dots are on a transparent backing and so solid lines show through.

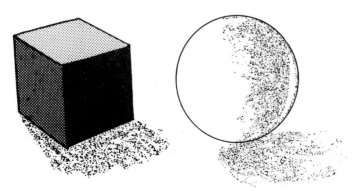

Instant textures

The tones in the examples above are printed on the film which is then cut and stuck onto the paper. Textures, though, are usually transferred from the film to the paper by rubbing on the back of the sheet. This allows for the creation of soft edges because excess tone can be cleaned off by scraping with a sharp knife, or lifting it off with sellotape.

The look of your book

The nature of the school's printer will dictate your options. Think flexibly! Could you have an outsize cover printed commercially with the contents printed by the school?

Books don't have to be based on a simple A sized rectangle. You can fold them in a number of different ways.

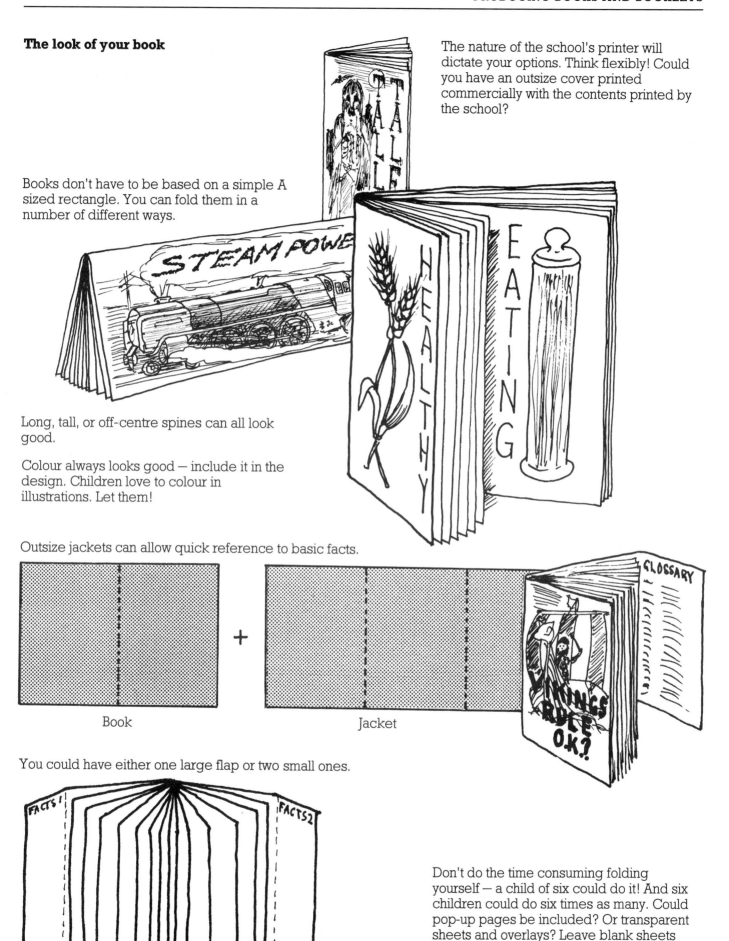

Long, tall, or off-centre spines can all look good.

Colour always looks good — include it in the design. Children love to colour in illustrations. Let them!

Outsize jackets can allow quick reference to basic facts.

Book + Jacket

You could have either one large flap or two small ones.

Don't do the time consuming folding yourself — a child of six could do it! And six children could do six times as many. Could pop-up pages be included? Or transparent sheets and overlays? Leave blank sheets for notes, cuttings and extra information. Remember that an A3 sheet will fold down to make a neat eight page booklet.

Binding your book

Books can be bound either temporarily or permanently. We won't consider methods of the former (which include things like ring files etc). But of the latter, there are five broad methods: staples, glue, clip on spines, plastic and spiral binders.

Staples

The ordinary classroom stapler and staples need no introduction from me. We all know their strengths and limitations. But there are now far more sophisticated staplers available, some of the electronic models of which can cope with around sixty sheets of paper at a time. These machines are a joy to use — many have a foot pedal, or electronic sensor which leaves the hands free to hold the work. The cost (about that of a small television) may put you off, but they are a sound investment for a busy school.

A book can be either edge stitched or saddle stitched. Of the two saddle stitching is much tougher and more sympathetic to being opened. Edge stitched booklets tend to fall apart when used heavily, even when the booklet has good quality card covers. The problem is that if you want a face size of A4, you will find that most in-house printing uses edge stitching. This is another reason for choosing A5: this can be printed on A4 sheets, folded and then saddle stitched.

Glue

The principle involved here is to spread glue (usually a hot melt glue) along the spine of a book, thus holding the loose leaves together. This is supplemented sometimes by an adhesive cloth tape. It is a form of edge binding, and, as anyone who handles old paperback books will know, will soon disintegrate if opened out flat. Rather curiously, this method is known as 'perfect' binding! With modern glues, the quality is much better, but it is still not really suited for school work.

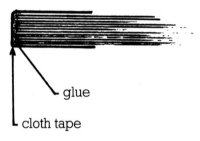

An earlier version of this kind of binding is still used for higher quality paperbacks and all hardbacks. It is known as 'sewn' binding. A number of slim subsections are sewn with threads which are then held by glue along the spine. It is seldom practical for books which are produced for use within a school.

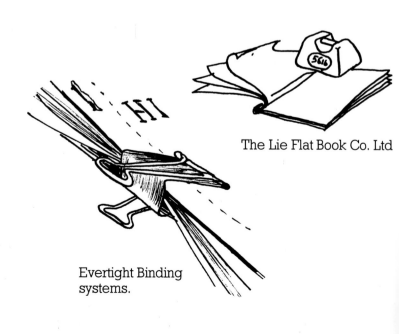

The Lie Flat Book Co. Ltd

Evertight Binding systems.

Plastic Binding

Under this heading we find two main types of binding.

Slide on clips

These are cheap and effective and a good alternative to ring binders. When coupled with a clear plastic folder, they are excellent for presenting essays. Their disadvantage is that they refuse to lie flat, and most people, when faced with one whose contents they are going to use extensively, remove it and deal with the leaves separately. If you plump for this method, make allowances with very broad spine-side margins. Choose the slide only after you know how thick the work is to be. Sizes, which come in a good choice of colours, range from 3mm to 17mm.

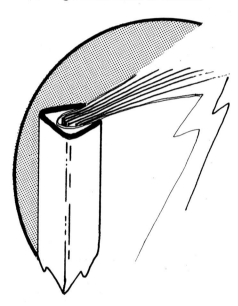

Their determination to stay shut, rather like windows at a post-office, count heavily against them.

Plastic ring binding

This is the most professional system available to us. It may be possible to buy the binding printed with your own title for a reasonable proportion of the cost of the work.

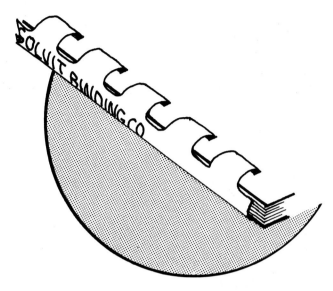

The result is strong and opens flat.

Spiral binding

This familiar system has similar advantages to plastic ring binding as it is robust and the book opens flat. Perhaps your school has a machine. If not, many of the 'instant print' bureaux will provide the service.

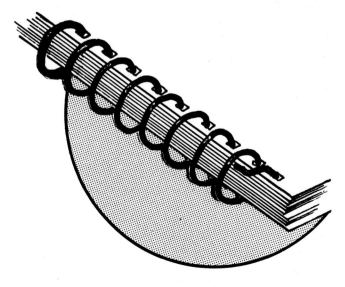

For the production of high quality, reference material these last two systems have no equal. They also work well at A4 size.

Use of colour

Full colour printing is a highly sophisticated process which can cost an enormous amount to set up. Each image has to be separated into different percentages of the four component colours; black, cyan, magenta and yellow. Each of the four colours requires a separate plate. Modern technology is making this easier all the time, so hopefully this process will soon become available for shorter runs and use in schools.

Colours can however be achieved in other ways, and with a little imagination we can have what is known as 'simple colour' or 'spot colour'. For example, it costs little extra to use coloured paper for some (or all) pages in a book. You can also print in inks of different colours. A swatch of 'Pantone' colours will show the enormous range of coloured inks which are available. You can print in coloured inks on coloured paper, with different combinations producing results which range from the elegant and sophisticated to the totally illegible.

If you wish to combine two or more coloured inks on the same page, then it is easiest to choose a design where the colours do not need to 'register' exactly. This example would give no problems to a printer and could even be produced on a two-colour photocopier.

Another way of adding interest is to print headlines and some illustrations in a different colour. As long as there is no need for a precise register, this is quite easy to do.

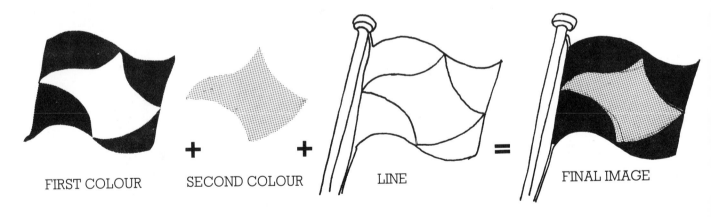

FIRST COLOUR   +   SECOND COLOUR   +   LINE   =   FINAL IMAGE

If a precise register is needed, then it can still be done, but everything needs more care and accuracy. Commercial printers do it as a matter of course, but if you intend to use an off-set machine in school, then some instruction and advice from someone with experience is invaluable. The line print should go on last, and if it is a good firm line with a deep tone, it will mask any minor inaccuracies.

So now we have looked at ways of producing books and booklets. In addition to books, you could try making school Christmas cards for charity. Or a school card which your headmaster can send to the school's friends. Sometimes, you may be able to produce a booklet on something that would interest members of the local community (i.e. Nature trail guides; Local history) which a local shop might be willing to display and sell for you. I hope that in this chapter I have convinced you that these enterprises have great potential for boosting your school's reputation and that the work is both interesting and rewarding.

THE SCHOOL IN THE COMMUNITY

How to promote your school in the local community

These days, even schools need to have good public relations. Your school may have a superb academic record. It may even have produced some of the finest synchronised swimmers in England. But unless you make a conscious effort to advertise your successes all your years of hard work will probably go unnoticed. This is heartbreaking for any of us who care for our jobs, and ultimately, it is bad for school morale and pride. This chapter looks at some cheap and simple methods which will enable you to promote your school in the local community.

On page 5 we saw a school entrance that was scarcely entrancing! A gate like this one here is not appropriate, or achievable everywhere, but is there anything you could do to improve yours? Perhaps the Local Authority would support a self-help scheme of improvement. Like the covers of a book, the entrance to a school can suggest the excellence which is to be found within.

A matter of communication

In recent years, many of our high street shops have been replaced by building societies. This invasion has seriously reduced the picturesqueness of our towns because there is very little a building society can usefully display in its windows. But in the name of public relations and goodwill, many managers have been happy to hand over their window space to people who are able to make better use of it. The alert teacher can exploit these new opportunities to help promote his school. Why don't you?

With a carefully calculated window display, you can effectively open a branch of your school in the high street. What easier way can there be to earn public esteem? There are so many of these possible sites that you may be able to be choosy. There are no hard and fast rules; use your discretion. But you should aim for a site with a good window, which is well lit, and which opens onto a street that is busy, but not so busy that it discourages people from stopping. Avoid sites that are potentially dangerous, and on the road to nowhere in particular.

Don't be surprised if you are put on a lengthy waiting list. If the bad news is that you have to wait a year, then the good news is that it is worth the wait. Why else would there be such a queue? Before you approach the manager, make sure you have a very clear idea of what you want. He is a busy man, and it is not fair to him to be vague and unbusiness-like. In the face of much competition, it may be best to adopt a brazen 'who dares wins' approach. Make use of any contacts you have (do you teach the children of any building society managers?) and once you have secured some window space, treat your benefactors thoughtfully. Perhaps your class could design a special 'thank-you card' which everyone can sign and send to the building society after the display.

POSSIBLE THEMES	POSSIBLE SITES	POSSIBLE AUDIENCE
<u>Advertising:</u> Plays Open Days Galas Musical or Sporting activities <u>Informing about:</u> New exams New internal arrangements (eg Pastoral structure) Policy changes	Building Society Bank Information centre Empty shop Town Hall	Pupils past, present and future Parents of children at feeder schools Townsfolk in general

In general terms, what are you going to put in your window? You may like to think of this as falling into two types: school information and school propaganda. There are (or should be in any active school) always events which need advertising: the swimming gala, the school play etc. Later, we will look at other ways of advertising school events, but if you have a window, you may as well use it for this.

School propaganda sounds rather subversive but what this means is showing off the school in a good light. Does your school get only a small fraction of the public into its Open days? This is a trend to be combatted. A good school must be approachable — after all, in a very real sense, it *belongs* to the community — and if there is really so little interest, then it is up to the school to create it. This is not done overnight, but a window display is a confident step in the right direction. People are much more inclined to judge by appearances, and a stunning display in the High Street can create a far more enduring impression than a list of GCSE results in the local paper. It goes without saying that if you decide to go ahead, you'd better do it well! A thoughtless, vapid display will do your school more harm than good.

Banks and tourist information centres are other possibilities. You can always ask! Shops are seldom going to give up valuable window space, but some may be prepared to hang a poster or a single item. Some bookshops, especially small ones run by enthusiasts, can be very co-operative in this direction.

This is a perfect site for a display. It is near a bus stop, with a broad pedestrian area halfway between the market and the library. The window is well lit by natural light, but is also equipped with special display lights and a power point. It is also equipped with the most helpful staff you could hope to meet!

The first thing a display must do is catch the eye. And having caught it, it must hold the onlooker's attention. This calls for all the tricks of the trade, and especially for clever use of scale. Learn from local experts if you can. Large stores often employ freelance window dressers, and you may well pick up some useful tips from an afternoon's window shopping. In my observation, good window dressing is infectious. If a town has one particularly good shop, then almost inevitably, the other shops have good displays. By the same token, some towns are uniformly bad. So if you are living in an 'uninfected' town, it will be interesting to see whether your display techniques catch on. The best way to hold attention is through 'human interest'. And if you can add some touches of humour to the display, all the better. But be careful — the number of people who can write and draw good humorous material is dwarfed by the number of people who think they can.

HEADLINE

HUMAN INTEREST

TECHNICAL DETAILS

Here are some ideas for 'human interest' strategies.

Photographs: People can't resist trying to find 'who they know' in a photograph.

Storyline: A frame by frame account of an activity or process.

Incongruity: Something out of place can grab the attention.

Comparisons: Groups of related items, especially 'now and then'.

A few permananent props can be very useful. A figure, like the one above can become a mascot. Items like this will often liven up an otherwise 'dusty' display.

The portable screens illustrated here are a real boon. They are used for displays in feeder schools as well as for windows in the town. Always do a 'dummy run' before setting up the display proper. Make sure you know the dimensions of your exhibition space, and then make sure your material fits it.

Arranging a display

Window dressing is very hard work. I, for one, sweat profusely when I set one up. But it is worth all the effort. If you have a strong nerve, you can hang around the display and gauge people's reactions. But the tension involved (will he? won't she? why on earth didn't they?!) may give lesser mortals a nervous breakdown.

We will briefly look at the main points again. You have chosen a suitable site and booked it. Now what sort of theme is suitable?

Themes:	facets of the curriculum extra-curricular activities local topics global topics something seasonal

Where possible, keep it simple.

Who is the exhibition aimed at? Remember that people of all generations will see your display, so plan it accordingly. When it comes to the design, remember the basic rules:

Unity:	The display must fit its setting. No matter how diverse the units, the final design must have a unity. There must be a sense of underlying order, but it must not be too regimented.
Contrast:	Experiment with light, colour, texture, size, broad sweeps and busy areas.
Light:	Allow for natural light, street lighting, and window illumination. Sodium lighting may destroy your effects (try reading a colour supplement under a street lamp!)
Space:	Remember the window plane. Gauzes can add to the effect of depth. Use the height, possibly through drapes (think of stage sets)

Colour:	Use it to distinguish between groups of objects. Try placing them on colour coded mats. Remember the seasons, in mid-winter you might like to aim for a warm scheme.
Backdrops:	Some shops won't want these, as they obscure their view of the street. Ask first.
Materials:	Beware of damp. As we saw earlier, this can be ruinous.
Credits:	Labelling should be clear and accurate. Give thanks for the loan of materials and the loan of the window.

Finally, let's run through some practical precautions.

Remember:	Do a dress rehearsal. If something can go wrong, it will! Have a 'first aid bag' with every fixative (and de-fixative) under the sun. Wear clean socks!

When you reach the site

Remember:	Clean out, and make your own backgrounds. Make frequent checks from outside. Fix lightly until you are satisfied. Final check: check everything one more time. Is everything the right way up as seen from outside? Are the levels and positions correct? Clean up threads, stray blu-tac, pins, footprints, the window surface etc. Be sure you can be contacted if the display needs attention and check it yourself periodically.

Do be prepared to respond to the outcome. The display, left, proved to be rather weak, but the flag saved the day. It provided a unifying background to counteract the dominance of all the horizontals.

Special programmes for special events

Good posters and programmes become souvenirs.

Make sure the programmes for your school's events are of the highest possible standard. Pictured on this page are a number of programmes which my colleagues have produced over the years. Apart from their aesthetic value, they represent an archive of the life and times of the school, and may in time become valuable memorabilia.

Before you go ahead with one of your designs make sure the roughs are approved by the people who are in a position to reject them. Different people have different opinions as to what is suitable, so avoid full blown artwork until you have the 'go-ahead'.

Using printed material

Well designed, headed notepaper is a silent statesman for the school. Why not design some? The P.T.A. may like to have its own notepaper as well.

Although they are easy to buy commercially, there is far more satisfaction to be gained if the school produces its own certificates. You can make sure they are appropriate to your school's curriculum. Remember that you can print onto coloured card or paper. Why not use instant-art for borders and school art work for the designs?

Sometimes material which is originally produced for class use or use within a school can be seen to have a wider potential audience. This nature trail guide was developed by a Primary teacher for his own class and then enlarged and revised at his local Teachers' Centre.

Edisford Primary School/Burnley Curiculum Development Centre

Banners

Banners can be a very effective way of advertising a school function. Not every event merits one towed behind the school Sopwith Camel, but a banner slung between two trees or across the street (you'll have to get permission for this) will usually suffice. The pictures on the right illustrate two different cases. 'Merrie England' is an expensive, one-off banner, whilst the 'Summer Festival' is an annual event and could have a reusable banner with a removable date panel. Banners are usually made out of tough calico or plasticised fabric and decorated with oil based paints. They also require very strong supports. Alternatively, could you attach a banner to some handy railings?

Inviting others into school

Many organisations would like to be invited into schools, and it is good public relations if you can set aside time and space for them.

They may bring their own displays (can you learn anything from them?) or perhaps you can put together a display to coincide with their visit.

Clitheroe 800 Committee

St Pauls Church, Low Moor

Not everybody is welcome!

84

HOW TO MOUNT A MAJOR EXHIBITION

Some teachers are born exhibitionists and some have exhibitions thrust on them.

This last chapter looks at the biggest manifestation of display skills of all — that of mounting a major exhibition. The value of one of these can be immense. Apart from showing off aspects of the school in the grandest manner possible they can act as strategic blows in the endless battle for more money. An Art and Craft exhibition, apart from a demonstration of the school's expertise, can be used as an argument in your struggle to squeeze a new kiln from the County Art Adviser. And if the headteacher is trying to cut back on your timetable allocation, a timely reminder of your good work may well persuade him to change his mind. A major exhibition is a first rate piece of in-service education and a market place for ideas. It is particularly valuable today, as we try harder and harder to share ideas across the curriculum.

The theme of such an exhibition ought to grow naturally out of work that is being done within the school. It is unethical to mount something with a 'School working for the community' theme if your school does (or did) nothing of the sort. But if the one improves and stimulates the other, perhaps it is churlish to complain. Use your discretion.

Some staff will be most eager to get involved, not least because they will share in the gains. But many others will be markedly less enthusiastic. It is, after all, a major imposition on their time, and they won't think to offer their help. This is not to say you that shouldn't ask. Do make sure before you start that the exhibition you are planning is well within the capacity of yourself, your helpers, your equipment and your materials and not dependent on white knights in shining armour turning up in time to save the day. In my experience, they don't.

"It's amazing the difference. You wouldn't think that it was the same child"

"I didn't know Kevin could do that"

"That project on the zoo visit seems to have really fired their imaginations"

"Yolande worked all week-end on those models for the maths table"

Whose work do you display?

This is more complicated than at first it might seem. It depends very much on the ethos of the school. It is an easy enough task to decide on the work you want, but in a school with a wide spread of ability, a core of gifted pupils may produce work that dominates the exhibition to the exclusion of those less able. Some schools regard this as symptomatic of life in general and accept it, while others may feel it encumbent upon them to give everyone a chance. And most take a view somewhere between these extremes.

However you resolve the dilemma, you can at least try to involve as many people as possible, even if some do no more than make cups of tea. Be sure to thank them publicly, whatever their contribution. Everyone likes to be appreciated and they may be encouraged to attempt more next time. An exhibition is a dialogue, so make it between as many voices as possible!

Who will see it?

The answer must be 'as many people as possible'. Apart from parents and friends, governors, relatives and children from other schools, don't underestimate the effect within your own school. Many children and staff will not be aware of the excellent work going on under the same roof.

Here we see an English teacher discussing an art exhibition before using it as a topic for written work. This cross-pollination of disciplines is an important benefit of large displays. If you are expecting your exhibition to be used in this way, then leave enough space for everyone to congregate.

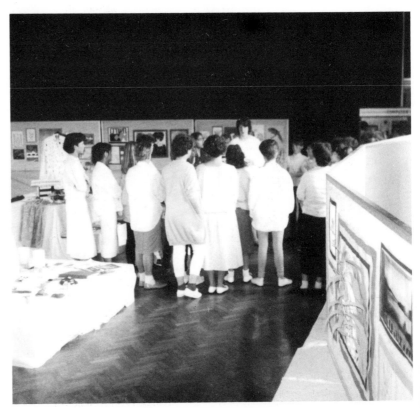

How can the exhibition be given unity?

Since by its very nature, an exhibition in a school will include work by many different people in different styles, there will be a need consciously to give it visual unity.

This can be done in a number of ways.

Colour: Could you use a common backing colour for exhibits on the same subject? Could you use a coloured band of constant width to head each related area?

Lettering: Does your school have a lettering style which people associate with it? If so, then use it for all headings. Don't forget to keep all headings the same size.

Logo: Graphic symbols are powerful reminders of connections and links.

Height: Commercial exhibitions often have a facia board of standard height across each stand to give visual unity. Could you achieve the same effect in any way?

Drapes at the front not only cover up unsightly table legs, but give the display a nice sense of unity.

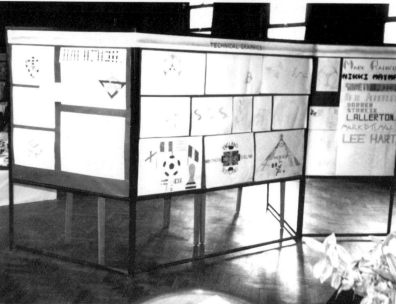

Here, a headband technique was used to unify the display. The clear space under the stands is a considerable aid to security. Legs and feet are a good indicator of the whereabouts of the arms and head!

Another interesting point to note here is scale. You'd be surprised how large lettering has to be for it to catch the eye. Check yours and do practical trials at an early stage.

Movement of people

Traffic flow can be a major problem in exhibitions, so think seriously about it. Most shows involve a logical progression from one stand to the next and you will have to think of ways of guiding people through it, and of roping off short cuts.

Perhaps you could have an introductory board at the beginning and a 'thanks for coming' board at the end. Use two main doors if possible and make it clear which is which. Perhaps you could start the exhibition just outside the entrance door and so draw people naturally in. If your exhibition is a considerable success, then you may need to think how to keep people moving through it. Once, an owner of a freak show improved the traffic flow by displaying the sign "This way for the egress". His visitors (knowing no Latin) assumed this was the prize freak of the exhibition and flocked out to see it!

Such measures are unlikely to be needed but you may well have a further room set aside for audio-visual resources, which support and augment the theme. Clear signing will help people to find it.

WAY IN

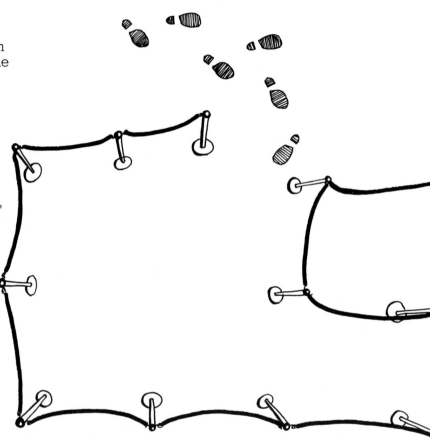

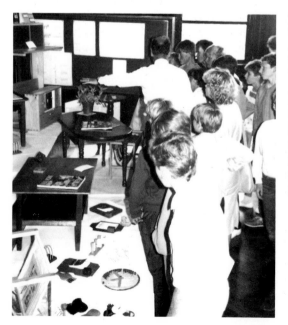

Dealing with visitors

To avoid conflict between rival school parties, organise a booking procedure. Make sure each party has ample time.

Make sure the guides know what is going on, and that there is always someone at hand to give an informed answer to an unexpected question. A display can be ruined by the guides, so choose and brief them carefully. They must be interested in showing the visitors what there is to see.

Producing a programme

A programme, apart from fulfilling its expected role of cataloguing the exhibits and giving out general information, is also a souvenir. And as such, you should endeavour to make it worth keeping. Don't forget that a programme advertises the school for as long as it is kept; an exhibition only for as long as it is remembered. And, vanity not withstanding, it says something about the person behind the exhibition. So, do give it an attractive cover which clearly shows the date, the name of the school and the theme of the exhibition.

The programme should start with an introduction which offers a warm welcome, giving a concise background to the show. There should perhaps be details of previous years' shows, and a discussion of developments and trends. And don't forget to invite the reader to ask questions of the guides and those children manning the stands. The more participation the better.

Illustrations

Any photographs or photocopies of the exhibition will be well received.

Plan

A complex exhibition will be better understood and digested if there is a plan.

Advertising

Some tasteful advertisements in the programme may well help to defray costs.

Follow-up

This is potentially the most useful section. It might take the form of a questionnaire which demands a more active response than usual. You could suggest items to be looked at, and also pose questions whose answers lie within the show. If the show is about a controversial matter, seek opinions about the issues it raises. The follow-up section is an opportunity to challenge ideas, and to propose starting points for class discussion, written work etc. If you do ask questions though, remember to give the answers. As always, setting follow-up work means that you must check it exhaustively to make sure it can be done.

The catalogue and credits

The simple rule here is: don't name anybody if you can't name everybody.

However much you intend putting in your programme, it should be possible to delegate sections of it to a number of different people. Once the system has been run once, it is relatively easy to change the dates and modernise it for future shows. The programme gives you the opportunity to invite visitors back next year, and once you have invited them, you have no choice but to mount another major exhibition!

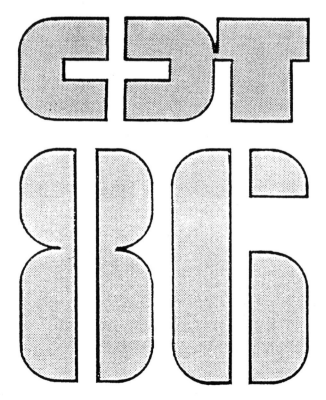

RIBBLESDALE SCHOOL CLITHEROE

CDT 86

An exhibition of work from the departments of

CRAFT, DESIGN and TECHNOLOGY.

Didsbury College of H.E.

Hospitality and staff co-operation

'Hospitality' is an important factor in the success of an exhibition. Apart from obvious things like cheese and wine (adults only!), lighting and music should be thought out. Some people will object to 'Musak', but it makes it harder to overhear things other people say, the fear of which may inhibit visitors from talking honestly.

Apart from fellow teachers, you should seek the co-operation of:
The Caretaker
The Office Staff
The Art Department
The Parents Committee
The County Adviser
Local Schools
The Teachers' Centre.
Cleaners

You will need volunteers for everything from moving furniture to providing refreshments. Often you will get the greatest help from people you scarcely knew before. But make enquiries about volunteers in good time. This will add to your flexibility and allow you to find replacements if someone is ill, or called away at the last moment.

Let other schools know about your exhibition well in advance. Otherwise they won't have time to book coaches and adapt timetables. See if you can build a 'grapevine' so that local (and not so local) schools freely exchange information about coming exhibitions.

Security should be planned. If you have valuable items on loan, they may have to be removed to vaults at closing time. You may even need security mirrors. The secret here is to arrange all the valuables so that they can be seen from one vantage point. Security is not only about theft, vandalism can be a greater problem. Any piece of work worth exhibiting is too valuable to risk getting damaged.

Check your display boards frequently for loose and missing pins etc. If not, the high standards you achieved on opening day will be lost. Perhaps you can arrange a regular patrol, checking up on all aspects of the show.

Finally, don't ignore the safety angle. Are all wires carefully taped or routed away from walkways? Is there a chance of heavy items falling? Does any of the staging need handrails? Don't forget that you are responsible for the safety of the school's visitors.

What about yourself? Are you insured to use a step ladder?

Count down to the big day

If your school has never mounted an exhibition, and you are worried about how to time your preparation, let's end with an imaginary run down to a major display. This scheme is the one I use, and it does work. With experience, you will develop your own, of course.

We are going to mount a major exhibition. So let's make a note in our diaries — no, not this year's, next year's! We'd better make sure it doesn't clash with anything (e.g. Wimbledon, the World Cup etc.). We must give ourselves at least one calendar year. The first thing we do is discuss it in outline with the Headteacher/Principal, and make enquiries as to the availability of the exhibition area, screens and display cases for the projected dates. If there are clashes, we must find new dates.
Book an in-town advertising area to co-incide with the eventual exhibition. This will provide excellent publicity when you need it. And finally, let's adopt a logo for all related memos and date them.

A fortnight has passed already. Time to invite staff to participate formally (perhaps we could have a meeting?). And all the while be collecting material and ideas.

Six months have passed. It's now time that we:
Order any expendible hardware we might require.
Send a memo to the staff who have committed themselves (reminding them about the show).
Contact any outside agencies to whom we might hope to offer space.

Three months later, it's time to check again:
Are staff still co-operative? Have any of the shirkers repented? Are the halls, screens etc. still available.
We should also arrange possible evening opening sessions, and liaise with the P.T.A. Now is the time to warn the Office staff etc. of impending work and to invite schools to send groups to the exhibition.

Six weeks to go. Time to arrange the use of the hall with the caretaker. Is there going to be an official opening? It is too late to book Joan Collins, but the Lord Mayor, or someone like him may well oblige.
Each contributor should now know what they are requried to produce. It's time to send out invitations (P.T.A., school governors, local M.P?), and produce the programme cover designs etc. We will also need a supply of P.D.N.T. (please do not touch) stickers. On the hardware side, are the drapes for the stands ready? Does the lighting work? Do we need any lightbulbs?

A month to go! It's now time to place advertisements in the local press (see if you can get local radio interested). The introductory notes for the programme should now be written, checked and typed. Let contributing staff have a plan of things like power points etc. Decide the space allocation. Be prepared to make changes.

A mere fortnight! Time to produce associated poster work, as much labelling as possible, information sheets etc, duty rotas for policing the exhibition (this may be staff, P.T.A., or students). Room changes, (if applicable) should be organised (and don't forget to allow for setting up time). We should now make out a list of exhibitors, check it and the programme notes, and pass it on to the office/resources for printing.

With a week to go, all possible setting up should be done.(e.g. start laying out display boards). Staff should know when they must set up their work. Tell everyone the expected number of visitors. Invite press and photographers.

We are into the final week. We must check and double check everything that we possibly can, will programmes be ready? Are all the staff still available? And if any invited schools have not yet replied, we ought to twist their arms a little.

Two days to go. Keep calm! The hall should be cleared, stands, tables and boxes set out. Make sure the screens conform to your colour coding schemes etc. Headings should be fixed ready for staff to set out their exhibits. The caretaker should be at hand to do any heavy cleaning. If staging is moved the floor may need attention.

During the day before the exhibition, everything should be completed. We should be able to go home knowing that everything is ready. Of course, if contributory staff fail to deliver, we must be ready to remove their screens or tables. If plants are going to be used, they must now be brought in. And we will check that the press is coming. Midday opening is probably easiest to handle, and it gives you time for the last minute alterations that shouldn't be needed. And if you have any spare time, give a guided tour to staff and children.

The big day — be there to welcome guests, offer programmes, and explain the purpose of the show. We must still keep checking to see that supervision is adequate, that the hall is locked at other times. It is an idea to record the event with photographs and videos.

After the show, everything must be carefully dismantled, and everybody must be thanked (personally if possible, but a note or card would be nice as well). Perhaps some of the material could be used again as a small travelling exhibition to take out to feeder schools and other places later in the year.

Of course, no matter how great a success the exhibition has been there will always be some points which could have gone better. That is the nature of such things. On balance we hope that all the hard work will have helped to make our school a more interesting place to be in and to provide a more stimulating environment for the children in our care. This was the reason for writing this book in the first place, and I hope that it will be helpful to you also.

The dust has settled.
There's one last thing we must do:

Sleep!

But we must remember to set the alarm — we only have a year to get ready for next year's exhibition!

BIBLIOGRAPHY

There are many useful books about various facets of display, the following have proved particularly relevant.

HERB CARITHERS	*Matting Techniques*	1978	P.F.E. Co. P.O. Box 10942 5839 N. Commerce Place Jackson, Missisipi 39206	*Excellent guide to picture mounting.*
QUENTIN CRISP	*Colour on display*	1938	Blandford	*Now very old but still relevant*
BOB GILL	*Forget all the rules about Graphic Design*	1983	Watson Guptill	*Full of great ideas*
NIGEL HOLMES	*Designers' Guide to Charts and diagrams*	1985	Watson Guptill	*Thoroughly relevant*
RITA KHON	*Experiencing Display*	1982	Scarecrow Press	*Rock solid basics, all line drawings*
JOHN LAING	*Do It Yourself Graphic Design*	1984	Ebury Press	*Full of processes, facts and technique*
JOHN LANCASTER	*Lettering Techniques*	1982	Batsford	*For the pure joy of lettering*
RAY MURRAY	*How to brief designers and buy print*	1983	Hutchinson	*All about producing books*
A. PLOWMAN/ V. PEARSON	*Display Techniques*	1966	Blandford	*Dated but very sound, shop windows 3D*
PLOWMAN/ MATTHEWS	*Animated Display & How to Get it Done*	1959	Blandford	*Fascinating*
GUNNAR SNEUM	*Teaching Design & Form*	1965	Batsford	*Very good for basic layout and lettering*
D. LETISSIER	*Instant Graphic Techniques*	1982	Graphics World	*The world of 'camera ready' art work*
J. TATCHELL/ L. HOWARTH	*Understanding Computer Graphics*	1983	Usborne	*A taste of the world of computer graphics*
B. THORPE	*Black & White Book*	—	Mirror Group Newspapers	*Free! Excellent guide to black & white illustration techniques*
VARIOUS AUTHORS	*Colour*	—	Mitchell Beasley	*Just about all you ever wanted to know about colour*

The catalogues of **Letraset** and **Mecanorma** are invaluable in themselves as well as showing the product range and how to use it.

The following publications are also worth looking for:

Graphics World eponymous bi-monthly publication and booklist, 7 Brewer Street, Maidstone, Kent ME14 1RU

Direction The Graphic Design organ of "Campaign, a monthly review of the world of advertising. 22 Lancaster Gate, London W2 3LY.

Dover Pictorial Archive Book Catalogue list of copyright free books. Art Publications Ltd., 28 Hardwick Street, Buxton, Derbys. SK17 6DA